# The Peeragogy Handbook

# The Peeragogy Handbook

*Founding Editor*

Howard Rheingold

*Managing Editors*

Charles Jeffrey Danoff and Charlotte Pierce

*Contributors*

Bryan Alexander, Paul Allison, Elisa Armendáriz, Régis Barondeau, George Brett, Doug Breitbart, Suz Burroughs, Teryl Cartwright, Joseph Corneli, Jay Cross, Karen Beukema Einstein, Julian Elve, María Fernanda Arenas, James Folkestad, Kathy Gill, John Glass, John Graves, Jan Herder, Matthew Herschler, Gigi Johnson, Anna Keune, Kyle Larson, Roland Legrand, Amanda Lyons, Dorotea Mar, Christopher Tillman Neal, Ted Newcomb, Stephanie Parker, Miguel Ángel Pérez Álvarez, David Preston, Paola Ricaurte, Stephanie Schipper, Lisa Snow MacDonald, Peter Taylor, Fabrizio Terzi, and Geoff Walker

Tuesday 20th October, 2015 (version $3.0\beta_5$)

The Peeragogy Handbook, 3rd Edition.
ISBN: 978-0-9855722-2-8

Cover art and illustrations: Amanda Lyons
Companion website design: Fabrizio Terzi
Layout and typesetting: Joseph Corneli

Typeset in Linux Libertine with XeLaTeX.
Sources available at `http://git.io/Handbook`.

Jointly published by PubDomEd and Pierce Press.

CONTENTS

# FOREWORD

I was invited to lecture at UC Berkeley in January, 2012, and to involve their faculty and their graduate students in some kind of seminar, so I told the story of how I've used social media in teaching and learning - and invited them to help me create a handbook for self-learners.

I called it the Peeragogy Handbook. I met twice on the Berkeley campus in the weeks following the lecture with about a dozen Berkeley faculty and graduate students. We also had a laptop open with Elluminate, an online platform that enabled video chatting and text chat, enabling people around the world who were interested in the subject, who I recruited through Twitter and email, to also participate in this conversation. All of the faculty and grad students at Berkeley dropped out of the project, but we ended up with about two dozen people, most of them educators, several of them students, in Canada, Belgium, Brazil, Germany, Italy, Mexico, the UK, USA, and Venezuela who ended up collaborating on a voluntary effort to create this Peeragogy Handbook, at peeragogy.org. We all shared an interest in the question: "If you give more and more of your power as a teacher to the students, can't you just eliminate the teacher all together, or can't people take turns being the facilitator of the class?"

Between the time nine years ago, when I started out using social media in teaching and learning, clearly there's been an explosion of people learning things together online via Wikipedia and YouTube, MOOCs and Quora, Twitter and Facebook, Google Docs and video chat, and I don't really know what's going to happen with the institutions, but I do know that this wild learning is happening and that some people are becoming more expert at it.

I started trying to learn programming this summer, and I think that learning programming and doing programming must be very, very different now from before the Web, because now, if you know the right question to ask, and you put it into a search query, there's someone out there on StackOverflow who is already discussing it. More and more people are getting savvy to the fact that you don't have to go to a university to have access to all of the materials, plus media that the universities haven't even had until recently. What's missing for learners outside formal institutions who know how to use social media is useful lore about how people learn together without a teacher. Nobody should ever overlook the fact that there are great teachers. Teachers should be trained, rewarded, and sought out. But it's time to expand the focus on learners, particularly on self-learners whose hunger for learning hasn't been schooled out of them.

I think that we're beginning to see the next step, which is to develop the methods – we certainly have the technologies, accessible at the cost of broadband access – for self-learners to teach and learn from each other more effectively. Self-learners know how to go to YouTube, they know how to use search, mobilize personal learning networks. How does a group of self-learners organize co-learning?

In the Peeragogy project, we started with a wiki and then we decided that we needed to have a mechanism for people who were self-electing to write articles on the wiki to say, OK, this is ready for editing, and then for an editor to come in and say, this is ready for Wordpress, and then for someone to say, this has been moved to WordPress. We used a forum to hash out these issues and met often via Elluminate, which enabled us to all use audio and video, to share screens, to text-chat, and to simultaneously draw on a whiteboard. We tried Piratepad for a while. Eventually we settled on WordPress as our publication platform and moved our most of our discussions to Google+. It was a messy process, learning to work together while deciding what, exactly it was we were doing and how we were going to go about it. In the end we ended up evolving methods and settled on tools that worked pretty well. We tackled key questions and provided resources for dealing with them: How you want to govern your learning community? What kinds of technologies do you want to use, and why, and how to use them? How are learners going to convene, what kind of resources are available, and are those resources free or what are their advantages and disadvantages. We were betting that if we could organize good responses to all these questions, a resource would prove to be useful: Here's a resource on how to organize a syllabus or a learning space, and here are a lot of suggestions for good learning activities, and here's why I should use a wiki rather than a forum. We planned the Handbook to be an open and growable resource – if you want to add to it, join us! The purpose of all this work is to provide a means of lubricating the process of creating online courses and/or learning spaces.

Please use this handbook to enhance your own peer learning and please join our effort to expand and enhance its value. The people who came together to create the first edition – few of us knew any of the others, and often people from three continents would participate in our synchronous meetings – found that creating the Handbook was a training course and experiment in peeragogy. If you want to practice peeragogy, here's a vehicle. Not only can you use it, you can expand it, spread it around. Translators have already created versions of the first edition of the handbook in Spanish, and Italian, and work is in progress to bring these up to date with the second edition. We've recently added a Portuguese translation team: more translators are welcome.

What made this work? Polycentric leadership is one key. Many different members of the project stepped up at different times and in different ways and did truly vital things for the project. Currently, over 30 contributors have signed the CC Zero waiver and have material in the handbook; over 600 joined our Peeragogy in Action community on G+; and over 1000 tweets mention peeragogy.org. People clearly like the concept of peeragogy – and a healthy number also like participating in the process.

We know that this isn't the last word. We hope it's a start. We invite new generations of editors, educators, learners, mediamakers, web-makers, and translators to build on our foundation.

Howard Rheingold<br>
Marin County<br>
January, 2014

# PREFACE TO THE THIRD EDITION

This 3rd Edition of the *Peeragogy Handbook* is dedicated to one of our most convivial – indeed, lovable – volunteers. George Brett was a quiet and learned man with a sense of fun. His mail art name was geORge and for a while he was known by many online for the selfies he took with his yellow rubber duckie. Far from being a full-time funster, George has been involved in expanding the educational uses of the Internet since before it was the Internet, both in his work with government institutions and his many online volunteer activities. He gifted the Peeragogy project not only with his knowledge and labor, but with his warmth and fun. We miss him.

The Second Edition of the *Handbook* came out two years ago. We've kept at it since then. This time around, we're kicking things off with a short workbook that contains a concise guide to the who, what, when, where, how and why of peeragogy. We've thoroughly revised the pattern catalog at the heart of the book, added more case studies, and made numerous small improvements to the text (and the typesetting!) throughout.

# Part I

# Introduction

CHAPTER 1

# WELCOME TO THE PEERAGOGY HANDBOOK

> We live where no one knows the answer and the struggle is to figure out the question. [1]

Welcome to the *Peeragogy Handbook*! We want to kick things off with a candid confession: we're not going to pretend that this book is perfect. In fact, it's not an ordinary book at all. The adventure starts when you get out your pen or pencil, or mouse and keyboard, and begin marking it up. It gets kicked into high gear when you join *Peeragogy in Action.* You'll find a lot of friendly support as you write, draw, or dance your own peeragogical adventure. But first, what is *peeragogy*?

Peeragogy is a flexible framework of techniques for peer learning and peer knowledge production. Whereas pedagogy deals with the transmission of knowledge from teachers to students, peeragogy is what people use to produce and apply knowledge together. The strength of peeragogy is its flexibility and scalability. The learning mind-set and strategies that we are uncovering in the Peeragogy project can be applied in classrooms, hackerspaces, organizations, wikis, and interconnected collaborations across an entire society.

The *Peeragogy Handbook* is a compendium of know how for any group of people who want to co-learn any subject together, when none of them is an expert in the particular subject matter – learning together without one traditional teacher, especially using the tools and knowledge available online. What we say in the *Handbook* draws extensively on our experiences working together on the *Handbook* – and our experiences in other collaborative projects that drew us here in the first place. The best way to learn about peeragogy is to do peeragogy, not just read about it. Towards that end, coauthors and fans of the *Handbook* have an active Google+ community, conveniently called *Peeragogy in Action.*

We maintain a regular schedule of weekly meetings that you're welcome to join. The *Handbook* includes a short syllabus, which also called "Peeragogy in Action", and you can work through this your own group as you read through the book.

You're warmly invited to combine your local projects with the global effort, and get involved in making the next edition of the *Handbook*. That doesn't necessarily require you to do extensive writing or editing. We're always interested in new use cases, tricky problems, and interesting questions. In fact, our view is that any question is a good question.

Here is a more detailed list of ways in which the current edition of the *Handbook* is not perfect. You're welcome to add to the list! These are places where you can jump in and get involved. We believe that airing our dirty laundry up front will give you a good idea of the issues and challenges we face putting peeragogy into action. If you're not intrigued by this sort of challenge, you might be best served by choosing a different adventure.

## Maintaining a list of useful resources

We include references and recommended reading in the *Handbook*, and there are a lot more links that have been shared in the *Peeragogy in Action* community. It's a ongoing task to catalog and improve these resources – including books, videos, images, projects, technology, etc. In short, let's "Reduce, Reuse, Recycle"! As a good start, Charlotte Pierce has been maintaining a spreadsheet under the heading "survey" in our Google Drive.

## Developing a really accessible DIY tool-kit

A short "workbook" containing interviews and some activities follows this introduction, but it could be much more interactive. Amanda Lyons and Paola Ricaurte made several new exercises and drawings that we could include. A more developed workbook could be split off from the handbook into a separate publication. It would be great to have something simple for onramping. For example, the workbook could be accompanied by video tutorials for new contributors.

Paola Ricaurte points out that a really useful book will be easy to sell. For teachers interested in peeragogy, this needs to be something that can be use in workshops or on their own, to write in, to think through issues. We're partway there, but to improve things, we really need a better set of activities.

The next time Paola or someone else uses the handbook or handbook to run a workshop, she can say, "turn to this page, let's answer this question, you have 10 minutes." There are lots of places where the writing in the handbook could be made more interactive. One technique Paola and Amanda used was turning "statements" from the handbook into "questions."

## Crafting a visual identity

Amanda also put together the latest cover art, with some collaboration from Charlotte using inDesign. A more large-scale visual design would be a good goal for the 4th Edition of the book. Fabrizio Terzi, who made the handbook cover art for the 1st Edition, has been working on making our website more friendly. So, again, work is in progress but we could use your help.

## Workflow for the 4th edition

We've uploaded the content of the book to Github and are editing the "live" version of the site in Markdown. For this and previous print editions, we've converted to LaTeX. There are a number of workflow bottlenecks: First, people need to be comfortable updating the content on the site. Second, it would be good to have more people involved with the technical editing work that goes into compiling for print. Remember, when we produce an actual physical handbook, we can sell it. In fact, because all co-authors have transferred their copyright in this book to the Public Domain, *anyone* can print and sell copies, convert the material into new interactive forms, or do just about anything with it.

## Translations

Translating a book that's continually being revised is pretty much a nightmare. With due respect to the valiant volunteer efforts that have been attempted so far, it might be more convenient for everyone involved to just pay professional translators or find a way to foster a multi-lingual authoring community, or find a way to create a more robust process of collective translation. Ideas are welcome, and we're making some small steps here.

## Next steps? What's the future of the project?

In short: If we make the Handbook even more useful, then it will be no problem to sell more copies of it. That is one way to make money to cover future expenses. It's a paradigmatic example for other business models we might use in the future. But even more important than a business model is a sense of our shared vision, which is why we're working on a "Peeragogy Creed" (after the Taekwondo creed, which exists in various forms, one example is [2]). No doubt you'll find the first version on peeragogy.org soon! Chapter 7 contains a further list of practical next steps for the project.

### References

1. Joshua Schimel, 2012. "Writing Science", Oxford University Press.

2. Taekwondo Student Creed, World Martial Arts Academy, `http://www.worldtaekwondo.com/handbook.htm`

Welcome to the Peeragogy Workbook! This booklet is designed to introduce you to our fun, exciting world of peer learning and peer production!!

You may already be familiar with these terms, or they may be new to you. Either way, **don't worry!!!**

If they are new, consider the following 2 examples.

1. *Peer learning*: Joe Corneli needs to get from the suburbs of Chicago to the north side of the city. He gets on the commuter train and transfers to the purple "L" at Davis Street in Evanston. He plans to change to the red line at Howard Street, but the train says "Loop" and he asks another passenger whether it will stop at Howard. She says it will, but that he can save an hour of his time by riding into the city and then riding back two stops!

2. *Peer production*: Two cavewomen see lightning strike a tree and produce fire! Walking up to it they notice the heat and think "Wouldn't it be nice to have fire for our family at night!" Once the rain clears, they find some

sticks and start working together to figure out how they can use them to start their own flame. After hours of trial and error, BOOM they've got fire! :)

Peeragogy is an approach to learning and working together on projects ranging from the mundane to the monumental. Peer learning and peer production are probably as old as humanity itself, but they take on new importance in the digital age.

The Peeragogy Project is an informal learning project with members worldwide. Three members of the project share their welcoming messages below.

**Lisa Snow MacDonald:** Welcome to peeragogy! It's kind of a weird name, but it's enormously powerful in providing to you some understanding of other ways of working together.

**Dorotea Mar:** Your contributions would be really welcome if you participate respectfully and harmoniously with other peers. It can change your life and improve your well-being and make everything better.

**Paola Ricaurte Quijano:** Welcome to the Peeragogy Project. We are a group of enthusiastic people that love to learn and are trying to find the best ways to learn together.

## a Peeragogy Interview

*Introductions*

**Paola Ricaurte Quijano:** Hi! I'm Paola, I'm from Mexico, I work at Tecnológico de Monterrey, a private university in Mexico City, and I love to learn to learn with everybody! So, I'm a superfan of Peeragogy!

**Dorotea Mar:** Hello. I'm in Berlin now and I really like the peeragogical atmosphere of collaboration and I think we are really improving ways of collaboration and peer production, so that's why I'm here.

**Lisa Snow MacDonald:** Hello. This is Lisa from Los Angeles. My background is media psychology and I'm interested in peeragogy as it relates to business.

*What is peer learning/production?*

**P** Well, peer learning. learning with peers, learning from peers and trying to make things together or make things happen together. I think that for me, the most important thing I've learned from this experience is that you can achieve more when you work together and set goals together.

**L** I think peer learning and peer production are unstructured ways for people to come together to pool their relative strengths to achieve results that might not be achieved if they were working individually on their respective sections and then trying to assemble them.

**D** I'm still trying to find out. i thought the answer to this question was clear to me when I joined the Peeragogy Project and then I realized there is so much more to this. When we're learning together there are so many other processes happening and they are integral processes of learning together. I think the answer is I'm still trying to find out.

**P** Yeah, I think Dorotea is right. I think that the process is the goal. And the emotional relationships that you build during the process are also important.

**L** I think what peeragogy does is it allows us to recognize the value of those connections. A lot of other ways of working are more individualized. It goes back to a concept of 1 + 1 = 2, which is very rational and very measured and is kind of a dominant way of thinking in our society today, whereas peer to peer learning and production recognize the value of those connections. You may not be able to measure it with a yardstick, but we understand that there is value in those connections. So it's basically acknowledging that when it comes to learning/collaborative environments if constructed the right way if working well it can be 1 + 1 = 3 or 1 + 1 = 4. That type of situation, which is really different from the way we're used to thinking about things. And I think that's really the value of what we're doing and the potential of what we could hopefully unlock.

*More specifically, what is peeragogy and/or what is the Peeragogy Project?*

**P** This is a project that began spontaneously. We didn't have a plan at the beginning. We just talked about the things that concerned us the most. What do you need if you want to learn with others, how to learn better? what do you want to learn? Where do you want to learn? When do you want to learn? Basic questions that can be answered in many ways.

We don't have a strict line. We have a map, maybe, but a map that can be walked through by many different paths. Paths that you choose can be related to the people you are working with. I think it's been a great experience for us. As Lisa said, we have been recognizing the talents and strengths of every person that has contributed and participated in this project.

**L** OK. I'll take my best shot with this. Going back to what I said earlier and building off what other people have said. Because we don't have a good mental construct in our heads as far of how this works and measurement is difficult. We haven't learned how to measure these connections.

I think what peeragogy and the Peeragogy Project can do is it can establish what people have said about focusing on the process. It can help people understand the process better. Because this lack of structure can be uncomfortable for people. We need to understand when that discomfort is acceptable, so they don't revert and become counter-productive participants in the process.

The map analogy is really good too that Paola just mentioned. It's not about providing a direct path. If you're on a trip trying to get from LA to Chicago, there's many paths you can take. It's making sure you're monitoring your resources and you're taking care of things along the way. You can drift off course. 1 + 1 can equal 0 if things don't work out well. So, what peeragogy and the Peeragogy Project can do is provide some structure and framework around the unstructured way that things can be done, so people trying to make sure it's constructive and beneficial have some guidelines and some things to watch out for.

### Example: Growing a Learning Network

**Howard Rheingold**: "When I started using social media in the classroom, I looked for and began to learn from more experienced educators. First, I read and then tried to comment usefully on their blog posts and tweets. When I began to understand who knew what in the world of social media in education, I narrowed my focus to the most knowledgeable and adventurous among them. I paid attention to the people the savviest social media educators paid attention to. I added and subtracted voices from my attention network, listened and followed, then commented and opened conversations. When I found something I thought would interest the friends and strangers I was learning from, I passed along my own learning through my blogs and Twitter stream. I asked questions, asked for help, and eventually started providing answers and assistance to those who seemed to know less than I. The teachers I had been learning from had a name for what I was doing — "growing a personal learning network." So I started looking for and learning from people who talked about HOW to grow a "PLN" as the enthusiasts called them."

**D** For me peeragogy is really a great experience. I think the way we do things we are going beyond any collaborative project basically. We allow so much freedom/openness in the Project. Everyone is welcome, basically.

Anyone can just jump in and propose something and this will somehow fit in. And this is quite amazing for me. Over the last year it will just be really creative. We don't really have any restrictions. People can join from anywhere in the world, like today I was cooking and that was OK. So I think that's really nice, the atmosphere, the relationships and the mutual respect we have for each other and appreciation. This is really important.

**P** I think that when we began this we were thinking about a new pedagogy of learning with others, so that's what peeragogy is, a new way of seeing and collaborating and learning in open spaces and spaces that are not constrained by time or space. It's an open learning environment for people that are driven by self-motivation of going somewhere with some others.

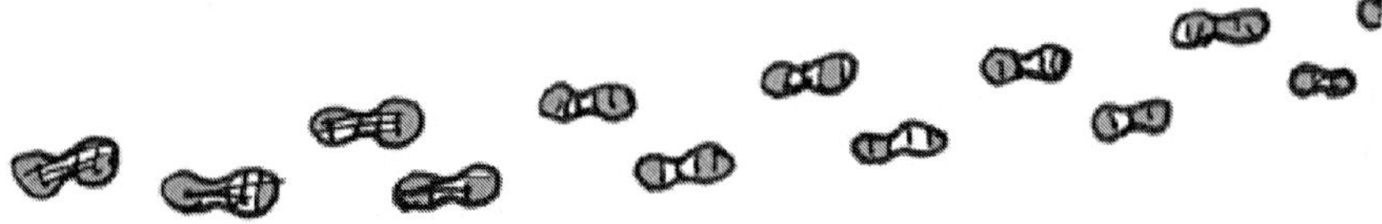

*How do you do peeragogy?*

**L** That's a good question. I've been thinking more about how you create a culture of peeragogy. It can tend to be a natural extension of the way in which people behave. If the culture/environment is created around a group of people they will tend to participate in that way. I'm not sure if you say I wanna do peeragogy I'm not sure how to respond to that actually. Except I'd want a loose structure, I'm not sure.

**D** I think I do a lot of peeragogy and I'm very happy about it because I learn so much from my group and from myself in this group that I like to apply it to other projects that I'm in or all the co-working/co-living projects or anything basically. Especially the principle of mutual respect that is still remaining after a very long time. And the really nice relating to each other.

The main principle is mutual respect and openness, mutual space not constrained by time/space. And the process. And what I meant by the details, in each detail there is value that we promote.

Let's say how we manage the Peeragogy Page or Community (See "How to Get Involved". These seem to be details, but they're actually really important. So if we pay attention to all these, every little thing matters, and this is how I do it. I try to be very careful about basically everything.

### Example: Learner, know thyself.

When he joined the Peeragogy project in 2012, Charles Jeffrey Danoff did a brief self-evaluation about what makes him interested in learning:

1. *Context.* I resist being groomed for some unforeseeable future rather than for a specific purpose.

2. *Timing and sequence.* I find learning fun when I'm studying something as a way to procrastinate on another pressing assignment.

3. *Social reinforcement.* Getting tips from peers on how to navigate a snowboard around moguls was more fun for me than my Dad showing me the proper way to buff the car's leather seats on chore day.

4. *Experiential awareness.* In high school, it was not fun to sit and compose a 30-page reading journal for Frankenstein. But owing in part to those types of prior experiences, I now find writing pleasurable and it's fun to learn how to write better.

**P** I think peeragogy is more like a mind-set. I think we have to change the way we relate to others and the way we understand the possibilities of learning. For example, I'm a teacher and, of course, my teaching practice tries to support collaborative, creative learning. So, I expect my students to take care of their own learning by making decisions about most aspects of the learning process. Program their own learning goals. The Blackboards, the environments they want to use. The activities and also the assessments.

I'm trying to give them conditions to decide how they want to learn and what they want to learn and how they want to learn it.

And for me it's been a very interesting experience. They are usually not used to making decisions about the process in a formal environment. At the beginning of the semester you give them everything and usually they just follow guidelines and criteria for the class. I have been trying with them to change this way of doing things. They feel insecure, because they really do not know how or what they want to do. So, that process of making decisions together is very rich and very meaningful for everybody.

**D** This for us was like a workshop so that we also learn how to be more peeragogical, and I think we're extending it to all the domains of our life. I think this is really nice, it's almost like we are self-coaching each other in being more collaborative and this is a very good thing for us, as well.

**P** As Lisa said developing this culture of collaboration in every environment and seeing every environment as an opportunity to learn together.

**D** I think we're also spreading the culture of collaboration in some ways and this is also very beautiful to do that. This is still an experience for us and we can also help to experience it by somehow interacting on what comes out of this project already and still is evolving.

The whole process of learning together. It was also a learning process for all of us and this group. I think so, I don't know how it was for you, but I feel like that. It helped us to create this culture of collaboration within our group and we have transferred it to other groups we are talking with. It became a light that is spreading all over somehow by different channels.

**L** I think what she said too is important, because we often don't have a lot of language and lots of words have double meanings. So when we look at the concept of team, it can carry with it different meanings. One can be disjointed approach where everyone has specific, different roles or there are other concepts of team where everyone is integrated and working together. And yet a lot of times those differences aren't communicated directly when you're working with groups. So we're bringing to the surface things that are often implicit when they're working in groups and by pulling it to the surface we're raising awareness that people are making choices and there are these different choices in how we approach things.

*Where do you do peeragogy?*

**D** Everywhere I can. Just now in the kitchen, cooking with a friend, I was doing peeragogy.

**L** I think you can do it just about anywhere. My interest though is as it relates to business. How different groups and departments work together.

**P** I agree w/Dorotea. I try to peeragogy everywhere. We should find a verb for that. I collaborate w/a group of human rights activists in Contingentemx (http://contingentemx.net/) and I also see my collaboration there as a peeragogical practice. When you are in a family you should understand you are a team, and if you don't see every member as a valuable contributor to the common goals of that team it doesn't work.

### Example: Metacognition and Mindfulness

**Alan Schoenfeld:** "What (exactly) are you doing? Can you describe it precisely? Why are you doing it? How does it fit into the solution? How does it help you? What will you do with the outcome when you obtain it? "

Schoenfeld, A. H. (1987). What's all the fuss about metacognition? In A. H. Schoenfeld (Ed.), *Cognitive science and mathematics education* (pp. 189-215). Hilldale, NJ: Lawrence Erlbaum Associates.

*When do you do peeragogy?*

**D** I think always. I really like that during the hangouts we don't have agendas usually. We just get creative. And whatever happens it's the right thing happens. We just work together and somehow the right things happens.

I think we're always doing peeragogy when we do things in open, collaborative, ways if we're not trying to restrict it with too much structure in the Hangouts or anything we do basically.

**P** I basically agree with Dorotea. The where and when questions are related. If you're thinking about where, you're thinking about when. So if where is everywhere, and then your when is also always, so I agree. Anywhere, everywhere, all the time.

It's an ongoing process. It's not something you can say NOW I'm applying peeragogy, but not for others. At least from my point of view.

If you believe in peeragogy in a sense in that sense that you believe in a way of doing things or making things happen, you cannot shuffle or break yourself into 2 people or 2 different persons and say I'm not working with peeragogy now. It's hard to split yourself in 2.

**L** In business there are personalities, and people who will tend to adapt and prefer a peeragogical model. They tend to be more collaborative just by nature. Other personalities are not, and that's why what we're doing here is valuable. There's often not recognition of these two different styles of working that's conscious. In a business environment it's not necessarily voluntary and people coming together united by a single goal. In biz you get different personalities tossed together, so understanding these rules and raising differences to the surface could be very valuable for the business to make other people's lives better in the business environment.

**D** To pick up on what Paola said about the process. Sometimes we like to think in our imaginations that Peeragogy is this, but then we realize that it's something more. It's like process within us and how we evolve this notion.

It means much more each time we refer to it. It's an evolving construct. The more we do it, the more we understand it and the broader we view the whole landscape around it and what really matters is how we do this and what other things matter. It's a process also in terms of our learning and understanding what it really is and it comes by doing it. It's learning by doing it's also evolving notion by exploring it!

**P** Yeah I agree with Dorotea in the sense that it's a dynamic, on-going process. It's very important to have the meta-cognition process. In the sense we are always reflecting how are we doing this? How do we want do this? What do want? Why? Are we doing the right thing? It's a long process in that we're always asking ourselves things. This process of asking ourselves questions is also a learning process. That makes us be more aware of things that should be promoted and things that maybe don't work that way.

*Who does peeragogy?*

**P** Of course, we consider ourselves the peeragogy team. Not everybody is familiar with our, let's say, strategies/beliefs. But I think, as we said earlier if we are feeling and thinking this a good way to solve problems and be creative, then it's a good thing to apply to any given environment. So it's difficult if other people, different from us, try to impose rules or define things without considering our ideas or input. Lisa was talking about organizations. I think they could gain a lot if they understand that peeragogy is a better way to work in an entrepreneurial or private environment, in general, I think it's good for all.

**L** I think a lot of people may not be aware of it who are working in that sort of environment. I think we all do to some extent. Going on social media, googling the internet for help on things, going into chatrooms can be a kind of peeragogy of peer to peer to peer support: a way of solving your particular problem. I think everybody does it on different levels, but they may not be aware of it.

**D** There are many collaborative projects that aim to do something of this kind, but they are not as much into it as we are in a sense. They notice something or promote something that we do also do not pay attention to other things that we consider important. Some people have natural tendencies to be peeragogical, and some people are not so transparent in the way they do things, but i think it's really beneficial, especially for collaborative projects. Everyone can learn a bit of that and do it if they bring more awareness to how they do things and what they think and not just focus on some part of it, but see things in a bigger picture in a sense, so I think people do it in little different ways and sometimes they do the opposite, but I think our role would be to bring more awareness to the details and process. And if people resonate with it they can say yes it makes sense and they can do it this way, but still I think it would help to focus attention on all that could be done in a peeragogical way, Bring more awareness to roles, would help to focus attention to all that could be done in a peeragogical way and maybe is not because there's not enough awareness of the process. In general my answer is most people are able to do it, but maybe they just don't know yet.

### Example: Setting Sail

**Jay Cross:** "If I were an instructional designer in a moribund training department, I'd polish up my resume and head over to marketing. Co-learning can differentiate services, increase product usage, strengthen customer relationships, and reduce the cost of hand-holding. It's cheaper and more useful than advertising. But instead of just making a copy of today's boring educational practices, build something based on interaction and camaraderie, perhaps with some healthy competition thrown in. Again, the emphasis should always be on learning in order to do something!"

*Why do you do peeragogy?*

**D** Because it feels really nice. It helps a lot with relating to people and evolving our relationships we have in projects and basically everywhere. It's a very healthy way of doing things and it makes us feel good, makes others feel good. I think it's a good thing in general.

**P** Why? Well as said before, I believe in peeragogy. I believe it's a good way to learn. Maybe it's the best way.

I think I wasn't aware of that before joining the group. I have always been a self-learner, I have been working mostly alone. After I began working with the group, I understood that you grow working with a group.

You achieve things that you aren't able to achieve alone. I think there's a growing awareness of the value of collaboration in every setting and environment. There are more and more learning communities everywhere in every place in the world that are also learning that are that doing things together and deciding things together is best way that you could be in this world! I think we are living in hard times so we need more and more the sense that we are not alone and that we cannot solve problems alone.

**L** My interest in peeragogy goes back to an experience in business and seeing the potential benefits of it an organization and seeing those benefits being stripped away as new executives came in and not understanding what they are stripping. I enjoy it, see benefits because I've experience it and seen how corrosive other ways of thinking can be to the well being of employees and the corporation.

*How did you join the Peeragogy project?*

**P** How did I join? Actually after taking Howard Rheingold's course on Mind Amplifiers back in 2012 he invited us to join this group. As I said before there was not a plan, just an open question of how to best learn with others. That's how it began. We had many sessions, discussing about many things. The Peeragogy Handbook (http://peeragogy.org) was the product of that process. We have been working with the Handbook, releasing new version every year and trying to see what would be the best way to go farther and what would be the future of our collaboration as a group/team?

**L** A couple friends of mine were involved in P2P learning. They were invited to a conference at UCI. Howard was at the event and they were familiar with him. We ended up in obscure classroom and he started talking about principles that were peeragogy related, while I don't know if it provided much value to my friends, it sounded a lot like what I saw in business and he mentioned the group. So after that, I spoke to you guys and, it's pretty random.

**D** I think many paths led to me joining it. I was doing research on Open Science and I have lots of academic experiences and I always wanted to improve the way things work and somehow I wanted to do it and make it more creative. I resonated a lot with the Peeragogy Project on many levels, so somehow I just joined, I think it was serendipity of some kind.

*This interview was conducted on December 15th, 2014. The transcript was edited. You can watch the whole interview online at http://is.gd/peeragogyworkbook_interviews.*

# Exercise: How do you see yourself fitting in?

**Potential roles in your peer-learning project**

- Leader, Co-Leader, Manager, Co-Manager Team Member, Worker
- Content Creator, Author, Content Processor, Reviewer, Editor
- Presentation Creator, Designer, Graphics, Applications
- Planner, Project Manager, Coordinator, Attendee, Participant
- Mediator, Moderator, Facilitator, Proponent, Advocate, Representative, Contributor , Activist

**Potential contributions**

- Create, Originate, Research, Aggregate
- Develop, Design, Integrate, Refine, Convert
- Write, Edit, Format

**Potential motivations**

- Acquisition of training or support in a topic or field;
- Building relationships with interesting people;
- Finding professional opportunities through other participants;
- Creating or bolstering a personal network;
- More organized and rational thinking through dialog and debate;
- Feedback about performance and understanding of the topic.

When you think
about Peeragogy
visually - what
do you think?
Send your
napkin drawings!!!

# How-To Get Involved in the Peeragogy Project

To join us, please say hi!

E-mail to:
peeragogy@googlegroups.com

Write to:
**Peeragogy Project**
c/o Pierce Press
PO Box 206
Arlington, MA 02476

Join a Google Hangout at 18:00 GMT on Mondays @:
https://plus.google.com/+PeeragogyOrgHandbook

We have multiple opportunities for peers to contribute. Here's our current "Top Ten" list:

1. Site: Google+ Peeragogy Handbook page
   - What happens: Coordinating Hangouts on Air, G+ news updates
   - Who's in charge: Charlotte Pierce & Charlie Danoff
   - URL: https://plus.google.com/+PeeragogyOrgHandbook/posts
   - Status: Active

2. Site: Peeragogy mailing list
   - What happens: Chance for newcomers to introduce themselves! Meta-level coordination for the project, main point of contact with the email-o-sphere
   - Who's in charge: Joe Corneli
   - URL: https://groups.google.com/forum/#!forum/peeragogy
   - Status: Active

3. Site: Peeragogy.org
   - What happens: Maintain the "master" copy of the peeragogy handbook, share public news about the project.
   - Who's in charge: Peeragogy Project
   - URL: http://Peeragogy.org
   - Status: Active

4. Site: Google Drive Peeragogy Work Folder
   - What happens: Hive editing, working drafts to be delivered elsewhere when they are finished or for final polishing.
   - Who's in charge: Peeragogy Project
   - URL: http://is.gd/peeragogydrive
   - Status: Active

5. Site: Peeragogy In Action Google+ Community
   - What happens: Random posts related to Peeragogy, quick communications between members, news about events, hangouts, etc
   - Who's in charge: Everyone
   - URL: http://goo.gl/4dRU92
   - Status: Active

6. Site: Peeragogy YouTube Channel
   - What happens: videos posted here
   - Who's in charge: Charlotte Pierce
   - URL: http://is.gd/peeragogyvideos
   - Status: Active

7. Site: Git.io/Handbook
   - What happens: versioned storage of the LaTeX sources for the print version of the handbook and other derived formats and scripts
   - Who's in charge: Joe Corneli
   - URL: http://git.io/Handbook
   - Status: Active

8. Site: Commons Abundance Network
   - What happens: Public facing landing page for the

accelerator, networking with other commons-oriented groups
    - Who's in charge: Helene Finidori
    - URL: http://commonsabundance.net/groups/peeragogy/
    - Status: Low Traffic

9. Site: Peeragogy Project Teams Google+
    - What happens: Meta-level coordination for the project
    - Who's in charge: Peeragogy Project
    - URL: http://goo.gl/AzxXQq
    - Status: Low Traffic

10. Site: Paragogy.net Wiki
    - What happens: You can find links to papers and books on paragogy and/or peeragogy.
    - Who's in charge: Joe Corneli, Charlie Danoff, Fabrizio Terzi
    - URL: http://paragogy.net
    - Status: Low traffic

Do not worry about rules or trying to catch up! Just jump in! :)

Visuals by Amanda Lyons (http://visualsforchange.com/).

Booklet by Charlie Danoff, Paola Ricaurte Quijano, Lisa Snow MacDonald, Dorotea Mar, Joe Corneli and Charlotte Pierce.

Prepared for Public Domain Day 2015 on January 1st, 2015.

CHAPTER 2

# CHAPTER SUMMARIES

## Motivation

You might wonder why we're doing this project – what we hope to get out of it as volunteers, and how we think what we're doing can make a positive difference in the world. Have a look at this chapter if you, too, are thinking about getting involved in peeragogy, or wondering how peeragogy can help you accelerate your learning projects.

***Case Study: 5PH1NX.*** This example focuses on the interrelationship of pedagogy and peeragogy in a high school English class, when students are encouraged to find and share creative ways to learn. Explore this case study for ideas and encouragement for your own learning adventures.

## Peeragogy in Practice

Here we describe some of the interaction patterns that we've encountered time and time again in the Peeragogy project. You can use the ideas in this chapter as a starter-kit for your own experiments with peeragogy right away. Sharing – and revising – patterns is one of the key activities in peeragogy, so you will likely want to revisit this chapter several times as you look through the rest of the book. Don't forget your red pen or pencil, because you'll also want to tailor the patterns we describe here to suit.

***Case Study: SWATS.*** We present another example of peer learning in a classroom setting, focusing on the process of improving overall student performance with the help of a group of student experts. After describing the case study in general terms, we then re-analyze it using our pattern tools to show how examples like this can be integrated into our project.

### Convening a Group

This chapter is about how to begin your own peeragogical project. You can also use the ideas described here to strengthen an existing collaboration. Simple but important questions will inspire unique answers for you and your group. In short: who, what, when, where, why, and how? Use this chapter to help design and critique your project's roadmap.

***Play & Learning.*** What makes learning fun? Just as actors learn their roles through the dynamic process of performance, In other words, the more we engage with a topic, the better we learn it and the more satisfying - or fun - the process becomes.

***K-12 Peeragogy.*** The key to becoming a successful 'connected educator-learner' involves spending the time needed to learn how to learn and share in an open, connected environment. Once you make the decision to enter into a dialogue with another user, you become a connected educator/learner and tap into the power of networks to distribute the load of learning. Depending on their age, you can even facilitate an awareness of peer networks among your students.

***P2P Self-Organizing Learning Environments.*** This section engages invites an exploration of support for self-organized learning in global and local networks. Emergent structures can create startling ripple effects.

### Organizing a Learning Context

Peer learning is sometimes organized in "courses" and sometimes in "spaces." We present the results of an informal poll that reveals some of the positive and some of the negative features of our own early choices in this project.

***Adding Structure with Activities.*** The first rule of thumb for peer learning is: announce activities only when you plan to take part as a fully engaged participant. Then ask a series of questions: what is the goal, what makes it challenging, what worked in other situations, what recipe is appropriate, what is different about learning about this topic?

***Student Authored Syllabus.*** This chapter describes various methods for co-creating a curriculum. If you're tasked with teaching an existing curriculum, you may want to start with a smaller co-created activity; but watch out, you may find that co-creation is habit forming.[1]

***Case Study: Collaborative Explorations.*** This chapter describes collaborative peer learning among adult students in the Master's program in Critical and Creative Thinking at University of Massachusetts in Boston. The idea in the collaborative explorations is to encourage individuals pursuing their own interests related to a predetermined topic, while supporting learning of everyone in the group through sharing and reflection. These interactions of supportive mutual inquiry evolve the content and structure within a short time frame and with open-ended results.

## Cooperation

Sometimes omitting the figurehead empowers a group. Co-facilitation tends to work in groups of people who gather to share common problems and experiences. The chapter suggests several ways to co-facilitate discussions, wiki workflows, and live online sessions. Conducting an "after action review" can help expose blind spots.

***The Workscape.*** In a corporate workscape, people are free-range learners: protect the learning environment, provide nutrients for growth, and let nature take its course. A workscape fea-

[1]Quick tip: if you create a syllabus, share it!

tures profiles, an activity stream, wikis, virtual meetings, blogs, bookmarks, mobile access and a social network.

***Participation.*** Participation grows from having a community of people who learn together, using a curriculum as a starting point to organize and trigger engagement. Keep in mind that participation may follow the 90/9/1 principle (lurkers/editors/authors) and that people may transition through these roles over time.

***Designs For Co-Working.*** Designing a co-working platform to include significant peer learning aspects often requires a new approach. This chapter describes the initial steps of converting an existing online encyclopedia project into a peer learning platform.

### Assessment

"Usefulness" is an appropriate metric for assessment in peeragogy, where we're concerned with devising our own problems rathan than the problems that have been handed down by society. We use the idea of return on investment (the value of changes in behavior divided by the cost of inducing the change) to assess the Peeragogy project itself, as one example.

***Researching peeragogy.*** This chapter is based on a "found manuscript" created by one of us as an undergraduate. It looks at the challenges that are associated with combining the roles of student, teacher, and researcher. It shows the relevance of peer support, and also illustrates the important factor of time in the evolution of an idea.

### Technologies, Services, and Platforms

Issues of utility, choice, coaching, impact and roles attach to the wide variety of tools and technologies available for peer learning. Keys to selection include the features you need, what people are already using, and the type of tool (low threshold, wide wall, high ceilings) used for collaboration.

***Forums.*** Forums are web-based communication media that enable groups of people to conduct organized multimedia discussions about multiple topics over a period of time, asynchronously. A rubric for evaluating forum posts highlights the value of drawing connections. The chapter includes tips on selecting forum software.

***Wiki.*** A wiki is a website whose users can add, modify, or delete its content via a web browser. Pages have a feature called "history" which allows users to see previous versions and roll back to them. The chapter includes tips on how to use a wiki and select a wiki engine, with particular attention to peer learning opportunities.

***Real-time meetings.*** Web services enable broadband-connected learners to communicate in real time via audio, video, slides, whiteboards, chat, and screen-sharing. Possible roles for participants in real-time meetings include searchers, contextualizers, summarizers, lexicographers, mappers, and curators. This mode of interaction supports emergent agendas.

***Connectivism in Practice.*** Massive Open Online Courses (MOOCs) are decentralized online learning experiences: individuals and groups create blogs or wikis and comment on each other's work, often with other tools helping find information.

### Resources

Here we present a sample syllabus for bringing peer learning to life, recommended reading and tips on writing for The Handbook, as well as our Creative Commons Zero 1.0 Universal (CC0 1.0) Public Domain Dedication.

# Part II

# Motivation

## CHAPTER 3

# WHY WE'RE DOING THIS

> Participants must bring self-knowledge and no small measure of honesty to the peer-learning project in order to accurately enunciate their motivations. If everyone in your peer learning project asks "What brings me here?" "How can I contribute?" and "How can I contribute more effectively?" things will really start percolating. Test this suggestion by asking these questions yourself and taking action on the answers!

Some of the primary motivators reported by participants in the Peeragogy project include:

1. Acquisition of training or support in a topic or field;
2. Building relationships with interesting people;
3. Finding professional opportunities by networking;
4. Creating or bolstering personal connections;
5. More organized and rational thinking through dialog and debate [1];
6. Feedback about their own performance and understanding of the topic.

We've seen that different motivations can affect the vitality of the peeragogical process and the end result for the individual participant. And different participants definitely have different motivations, and the differences can be surprising: for instance, if you're motivated by social image, you may not be so interested in reciprocity, and vice versa [2]. Motivations come with associated risks. For example, one may be reluctant to mention business aspirations in a volunteer context for fear of seeming greedy or commercial. Whether or not potential peeragogues eventually decide to take on the risk depends on various factors. Actions that typify inappropriate behavior in one culture might represent desirable behavior in another. Motivations often come out of the closet through conflict; for example, when one learner feels offended or embarrassed by the actions of another.

When it comes to primary motivators, it seems some people are more motivated by the *process* and some people are motivated by the *end result.* A lot of the motivations mentioned in the list above are process-oriented. A process orientation is exemplified in the following quote:

> **Philip Spalding**: "The idea of visiting a garden together in a group to learn the names of flowers might have been the original intention for forming a Garden Group. The social aspect of having a day out might be goal of the people participating."

The basic dichotomy between process and product can be a source of tension. Some people are OK with a process that is long and drawn out – because they're mostly there for the process itself anyway. Others will only tolerate with a slight delay as long as the important end result remains in sight. Without a clear understanding and a good balance between these different core motivators, there will be conflict.

People often come to a collaboration with their own motivation in mind (with more or less clarity from case to case). They don't always step back to realise that other people are coming from the point of view of another often very different motivation. It never hurts to ask, especially when conflict rears up. Accordingly, especially for those readers who are interested in the *end results* and *applications* of peeragogy, and not yet steeped in the process, here's what we ask:

*What are the problems you're grappling with? How do you think "peer learning" and "peer production" could help you? Would you be willing to share some of the techniques that you use, and to learn together with us?*

## Example: Peeragogy editor Charlotte Pierce

Basically, I'm here because as an early adopter and admitted gadget freak, I find it fun and rewarding to explore new technologies and topics that I feel have a practical or exciting application. But I have some some other motivations that subtly co-exist alongside my eagerness to explore and learn.

Howard Rheingold's reputation as an innovator and internet pioneer got my attention when he announced his Think-Know Tools course on Facebook in 2012. I had known of Howard from the 1990's when I was a member of The WELL (Whole Earth 'Lectronic Link). I was curious to see what Howard was up to, so I signed onto the wiki site, paid my $300, and took the course starting in October.

Looking back, I realize we were practicing Peeragogy throughout the TKT course, though at the time I hardly knew peer learning from a pickle. In late November, missing the camaraderie and challenge of TKT, I stepped over to check out the *Peeragogy Handbook*.

Which brings me to motivations in signing on to Peeragogy. Since Howard and several Think-Know Tools co-learners were already dedicating their time here and their work looked innovative and exciting, I suspected they might be onto something that I wanted to be a part of. Plus, my brain was primed by the TKT experience. "What if a diverse group of people could learn a subject with little or no cost and not a lot of barriers to entry," I thought. "What if their own experience qualified them to join, contribute, and learn."

I also thought there might be a chance to meet some potential business partners or clients there - but if not, the experience looked rewarding and fun enough for me to take the risk of no direct remuneration. There was no up front cost to me, and a wealth of knowledge to gain as a part of something new and exciting. These are always big draws for me. I wanted to be in on it, and nobody was telling me I couldn't!

My projections proved correct. The participants already on board were gracious in welcoming me to Peeragogy, patient in getting me up to speed, and persistent in coaxing me into using the tools central to the project. I connected, learned, grew, and contributed. Now I'm on the brink of starting a peer learning project of my own in my publishing organization, IPNE.org. Stay tuned!

## Example: Cafes, schools, workshops

Suppose we wanted to make Peeragogy into a model that can be used in schools, libraries, and so forth, worldwide - and, in fact we do! How can we bring the basic Peeragogy motivations to bear, and make a resource, plan of action, and process that other people can connect with? In brief, how do we build peer learning into the curriculum, providing new insight from the safety of the existing structure?

One concrete way to implement these broad aims would be to make a peeragogy-oriented *development* project whose goal is to set up a system of internet cafes, schools, or workshops in places like China or Africa, where people could go to collaborate on work or to learn technical subjects. Students could learn on the job. It seems reasonable to think that investors could make a reasonable profit through "franchises," hardware sales, and so forth – and obviously making money is a motivation that most people can relate to.

In developing such a project, we would want to learn from other similar projects that already exist. For example, in Chicago, State Farm Insurance has created a space called the "Next Door Cafe" that runs community events. One of their offerings is free financial coaching, with the explicit agreement that the issues you discuss return to State Farm as market research.

> **State Farm Insurance**: "Free? Really. Yes, because we're experimenting. We want to learn what people really want. Then, we'll shoot those wants back to the

Farm. We help you. You help us innovate. We're all smarter for it. We think it's a win-win."

Thus, Next Door Cafe forms part of a system to exploit the side-effects of interpersonal interactions to create a system that learns. A peer learning example from the opposite side of the world started in a slum next to New Delhi where Sugata Mitra gave children a computer and they self organized into a learning community and taught themselves how to use the machine and much more.

> **Sugata Mitra**: "I think what we need to look at is we need to look at learning as the product of educational self-organization. If you allow the educational process to self-organize, then learning emerges. It's not about making learning happen. It's about letting it happen."

In 2014, we tried a similar experiment. We asked: Can we build a "Peeragogy Accelerator" for a half-dozen peer learning projects, each of which defines their own metrics for success, but who come together to offer support and guidance, using the *Peeragogy Handbook* as a resource? We tried that with several our own projects, and benefitted from the peer support. Several months later, we found the Accelerator format even more exciting when we ran a one-off series focusing on Sagarika Bhatta's research on adaptation to climate change in Nepal. Our sense is that peeragogy could be useful for building a global support network around just about any project. Peeragogy can support a culture of real engagement, rather than "clicktivism," and the direct exchange of critically-assessed effort rather than often-inefficient donations of cash [3].

## References

1. Hugo Mercier and Dan Sperber (2011). Why do humans reason? Arguments for an argumentative theory, *Behavioral and Brain Sciences*, 34, 57-111.

2. Jérôme Hergueux (2013). Cooperation in a Peer Production Economy: Experimental Evidence from Wikipedia, talk presented at the Berkman Center for Internet and Society.
3. Kevin Edmonds (2012). Beyond Good Intentions: The Structural Limitations of NGOs in Haiti. *Critical Sociology*, 39(3).

CHAPTER 4

# CASE STUDY: 5PH1NX

David Preston

> 5PH1NX: 5tudent Peer Heuristic for 1Nformation Xchange - we think of it as a "curiously trans-media" use case in peeragogical assessment.

Over the last several decades technology has driven massive shifts in the way we communicate and collaborate. Information technology, socioeconomic trends, an increasingly complex and uncertain future, and school's failed brand are contributing factors in an emerging discourse that seeks to align learning with our rapidly changing culture.

Open Source Learning and Peeragogy, two emerging theoretical frameworks in this discourse, leverage end-to-end user principles of communication technology to facilitate peers learning together and teaching each other. In both traditional and liminal learning communities, one of the major points of contact between education and societal culture is the purposeful use of assessment. The processes of giving, receiving, and applying constructive critique makes learners better thinkers, innovators, motivators, collaborators, coworkers, friends, relatives, spouses, teammates, and neighbors. Implementing peer-based assessment can be problematic in schooling institutions where evaluative authority is traditionally conflated with hierarchical authority, and where economic and political influences have focused attention on summative, quantitative, standardized measurement of learning and intelligence.

This is the story of how one learning community is adopting Open Source Learning and Peeragogical principles to decentralize and enrich the assessment process.

> **Aldous Huxley**: "Knowledge is acquired when we succeed in fitting a new experience into the system of concepts based upon our old experiences. Understanding comes when we liberate ourselves from the old and so make possible a direct, unmediated contact with the new, the mystery, moment by moment, of our existence."

## Enter 5PH1NX

On Monday, April 2, 2011, students in three English classes at a California public high school discovered anomalies in the day's entry on their course blog. (Reminder: not so long ago this sentence would have been rightly interpreted as being science fiction.) The date was wrong and the journal topic was this:

> In The Principles of Psychology (1890), William James wrote, "The faculty of voluntarily bringing back a wandering attention, over and over again, is the very root of judgment, character and will. No one is *compos sui* if he have it not. An education which should improve this faculty would be the education par excellence." How have your experiences in this course helped you focus your attention? What do you still need to work on? What elements of the following text (from Haruki Murakami's *1Q84*) draw your attention and help you construct meaning?
>
> The driver nodded and took the money. "Would you like a receipt?" "No need. And keep the change." "Thanks very much," he said. "Be care**f**ul, it looks windy out there. Don't sl**i**p." "I'll be careful," Aomame said. "A**n**d also," the **d**river said, facing **t**he mirror, "please remember: t**h**ings are not what they seem." Things are not what they seem, Aomame repeated mentally. "What do you mean by that?" she asked with knitt**e**d brows. The driver chose his words

carefully: "It's **j**ust that y**o**u're about to do something out of the ordinary. Am I right? People do not ordinarily climb down the emergency stairs of the Metropolitan Expressway in the middle of the day–especially women." "I suppose you're right." "Right. And after you do something like that, the everyday loo**k** of things might seem to chang**e** a little. Things may look *different* to you than they did before. I've had that experience myself. But don't let appearance**s** fool you. There's always only one reality."

## Find the jokers

The jokers were real and hidden (without much intent to conceal) around the classroom and in students' journals. Students found them and asked questions about the letters in bold; the questions went unanswered. Some thought it was just another of their teacher's wild hair ideas. Although they didn't know it yet they were playing the liminal role that Oedipus originated in mythology. Solving the riddle would enable them to usher out an old way of thinking and introduce the new.

The old way: An authority figure sets the rules, packages the information for a passive audience, and unilaterally evaluates each learner's performance. In that context, peeragogical assessment might be introduced with a theoretical framework, a rubric, and a lesson plan with input, checks for understanding, and guided practice as a foundation for independent work.

The new way: In Open Source Learning the learner pursues a path of inquiry within communities that function as end-to-end user networks. Each individual begins her learning with a question and pursues answers through an interdisciplinary course of study that emphasizes multiple modalities and the five Fs: mental Fitness, physical Fitness, spiritual Fitness, civic Fitness, and technological Fitness. Learners collaborate with mentors and receive feedback from experts, community-based peers, and the public. They are the heroes of learning journeys. Heroes don't respond to syllabi. They respond to calls to adventure. Open Source Learning prepares students for the unforeseen.

By the time they met the 5PH1NX students had learned about habits of mind, operating schema, digital culture and community, self-expression, collaboration, free play, autonomy, confidence/trust/risk, and resilience. These ideas had been reinforced through nonfiction articles and literary selections such as Montaigne's Essays, Plato's Allegory of the Cave, Shakespeare's Hamlet, Sartre's No Exit and others. The first poem assigned in the course was Bukowski's "Laughing Heart". *The Gods will offer you chances. Know them. Take them.*

So it is with knowledge and understanding. Today we are presented with an overwhelming, unprecedented quantity and variety of data in our physical and virtual lives; to cope we must improve the ways we seek, select, curate, analyze, evaluate, and act on information.

On the back of each Joker card was a QR code that linked to a blog page with riddles and clues to a search. At this point students realized they were playing a game. A tab on the blog page labeled "The Law" laid out the rules of engagement:

## This is The Law

1. You cannot "obey" or "break" The Law. You can only make good decisions or bad decisions.
2. Good decisions lead to positive outcomes.
3. Bad decisions lead to suffering.
4. Success requires humanity.
5. "For the strength of the Pack is the Wolf, and the strength of the Wolf is the Pack." -Rudyard Kipling
6. "The Way of the sage is to act but not to compete." -Lao Tzu
7. Be honorable.
8. Have fun.
9. Question.
10. *Sapere aude.*

This is The Law. After a second set of on-campus and blog quests, students noticed a shift in 5PH1NX. A couple of weeks before the first clue was published, during a Socratic seminar on Derrida's concept of Free Play, a student said, "We learn best when adults take away the crutches and there is no safety net."? The quote was used in the next clue; students began to realize that the game was not pre-determined. 5PH1NX was evolving in response to their contributions. This is a manifestation of the hackneyed writing cliché: show, don't tell. The student's comment was a call to action. The Feats of Wisdom were designed to engage learners over a vacation break in fun, collaborative, social media-friendly missions that required engagement in the community, expansion of their personal learning networks, and documentation on their blogs. For example:

**FEAT #1.** *Buy a ticket to "The Hunger Games" (or any other movie that's likely to draw a large, young, rowdy audience). Before the lights dim and the trailers begin, walk to the screen, turn to the audience, and in a loud, clear voice, recite the "To be, or not to be..." soliloquy from Hamlet (don't worry if you make a couple mistakes, just be sure you make it all the way to, "Be all my sins remembered."). Capture the event on video & post it to your blog.*

Students had been using the Internet without an Acceptable Use Policy all year; such policies are one-to-many artifacts of a central authority and far weaker than community norms. So rather than introduce "rules" 5PH1NX simply provided a reminder of the client-side responsibility.

## The Emergence of Peeragogical Assessment

The third page on the Feats of Wisdom blog was entitled *Identifying and Rewarding Greatness*, where learners were greeted with the following paragraph:

> If you see something that was done with love, that pushed the boundaries, set the standard, broke the mold, pushed the envelope, raised the bar, blew the doors off, or rocked in some previously unspecified way, please bring it to the attention of the tribe by posting a link to it [here].

No one did. Instead, they started doing something more effective. They started building. One student hacked the entire game and then created her own version. Other students began to consider the implications for identifying and rewarding greatness. They realized that one teacher couldn't possibly observe how 96 students were working over vacation out in the community and online to accomplish the Feats of Wisdom. In order to get credit for their efforts they would have to curate and share their work-process and product. They also realized that the same logic applied to learning and coursework in general; after all, even the most engaged, conscientious teacher only sees a high school or college student a few hours a week, under relatively artificial conditions. The learner presumably spends her whole life in the company of her own brain. Who is the more qualified reporting authority? With these thoughts in mind students created *Project Infinity*, a peer-to-peer assessment platform through which students could independently assign value to the thoughts and activities they deemed worthy. Because the 2011-12

5PH1NX was a three-week exercise in gamification, *Project Infinity* quickly evolved to include collaborative working groups and coursework. This was learner-centered Peeragogical assessment in action; learners identified a need and an opportunity, they built a tool for the purpose, they managed it themselves, and they leveraged it in a meaningful way to support student achievement in the core curriculum.

## Project Infinity 2 & Implications for the Future

Alumni from the Class of 2012 felt such a strong positive connection to their experience in Open Source Learning and Peeragogical assessment that they built a version for the Class of 2013. They created *Project Infinity 2* with enhanced functionality. They asked the teacher to embed an associated Twitter feed on the course blog, then came to classes to speak with current students about their experiences. Everyone thought the Class of 2013 would stand on the shoulders of giants and adopt the platform with similar enthusiasm. They were wrong. Students understood the concept and politely contributed suggestions for credit, but it quickly became evident that they weren't enthusiastic. Submissions decreased and finally the *Project Infinity 2* Twitter feed disappeared from the course blog. Learners' blogs and project work suggested that they were mastering the core curriculum and meta concepts, and they appeared generally excited about Open Source Learning overall. So why weren't they more excited about the idea of assessing themselves and each other? Because *Project Infinity 2* wasn't theirs. They didn't get to build it. It was handed to them in the same way that a syllabus is handed to them. No matter how innovative or effective it might be, *Project Infinity 2* was just another tool designed by someone else to get students to do something they weren't sure they wanted or needed to do in the first place. Timing may also be a factor. Last year's students didn't meet 5PH1NX until the first week in April, well into the spring semester. This year's cohort started everything faster and met 5PH1NX in November. In January they understood the true potential of their situation started to take the reins. As students realized what was happening with the clues and QR codes they approached the teacher and last year's alumni with a request: "Let Us In." They don't just want to design learning materials or creatively demonstrate mastery, they want to chart their own course and build the vehicles for taking the trip. Alumni and students are becoming Virtual TAs who will start the formal peer-to-peer advising and grading process. In the Spring Semester all students will be asked to prepare a statement of goals and intentions, and they will be informed that the traditional teacher will be responsible for no more than 30% of their grade. The rest will come from a community of peers, experts and members of the public. On Tuesday of Finals Week, 5PH1NX went from five players to two hundred. Sophomores and freshman have jumped into the fray and hacked/solved one of the blog clues before seniors did. Members of the Open Source Learning cohort have also identified opportunities to enrich and expand 5PH1NX. A series of conversations about in-person retreats and the alumni community led to students wanting to create a massively multiple player learning cohort. Imagine 50,000-100,000 learners collaborating and sharing information on a quest to pass an exam by solving a puzzle that leads them to a "Learning Man Festival"? over Summer break. When 5PH1NX players return from Winter Break in January they will transform their roles relative to the game and the course. Several have already shared "AHA!" moments in which they discovered ways to share ideas and encourage collaboration and peer assessment. They have identified Virtual Teaching Assistant candidates, who will be coached by alumni, and they have plans to provide peer-based assessment for their online work. They are also now actively engaged in taking more control over the collaboration process itself. On the last day of the semester, a post-finals throwaway day of 30-minute class sessions that administrators put on the calendar to collect Average Daily Attendance money, hardly anyone came to campus. But Open Source Learning students were all there. They have separated the experience of learning from the temporal, spatial, and cultural constraints of school. They understand how democracy works: those who participate make the decisions. No one knows how this ends, but the outcome of Peeragogical assessment is not a score; it is learners who demonstrate their thinking progress and mastery through social production and peer-based critique. This community's approach to learning and assessment has prepared its members for a complex and uncertain future by moving them from a world of probability to a world of possibility. As one student put it in a video entitled "We Are Superman," "What we are doing now may seem small, but we are part of something so much bigger than we think. What does this prove? It proves everything; it proves that it's possible."

## Background

A world in which work looks like what's described in the PSFK think tank's *Future of Work Report 2013* requires a new learning environment.

The problem is that tools and strategies such as MOOCs, videos, virtual environments, and games are only as good as the contexts in which they are used. Even the most adept practitioners quickly discover that pressing emerging technology and culture into the shape of yesterday's curricular and instructional models amounts to little more than Skinner's Box 2.0. So what is to be done? How can we use emerging tools and culture to deliver such an amazing individual and collaborative experience that it shatters expectations and helps students forget they're in school long enough to fall in love with learning again?

Education in the Information Age should enable learners to find, analyze, evaluate, curate, and act on the best available information. Pursuing an interdisciplinary path of inquiry in an interest-based community doesn't just facilitate the acquisition of factual knowledge (which has a limited half-life). The process brings learners closer to understanding their own habits of mind and gives them practice and an identity in the culture they'll be expected to join after they graduate. This requires new literacies and a curriculum that emphasizes mental fitness, physical fitness, spiritual fitness, civic fitness, and technological fitness.

Models of assessment that emphasize self-directed and collaborative Peeragogical principles enrich the learning experience and accelerate and amplify deep understanding. Because these approaches are pull-based and generate tens of thousands of multi- or trans-media data points per learner, they also generate multi-dimensional portraits of learner development and provide feedback that goes far beyond strengths and weaknesses in content retention. The long-term benefit is exponential. Learners who can intentionally direct their own concentration are empowered far beyond knowledge acquisition or skill mastery. They become more effective thinkers and – because they are invested – more caring people. This learning experience is of their own making: it isn't business, it's personal. The inspiration to recreate the process for themselves and for others is the wellspring of the lifelong learner.

As Benjamin Disraeli put it, "In general the most successful man in life is the man who has the best information." It is a widely accepted truism in business that better data leads to better decisions. We now have the ability to generate, aggregate, analyze, and evaluate much richer data sets that can help us learn more about helping each other learn. Sharing richer data in different ways will have the same game changing effect in learning that it has in professional sports and investment banking.

Self-directed, collaborative assessment generates an unprecedented quantity and variety of data that illuminates aspects of learning, instruction, and overall systemic efficacy. Even a quick look at readily available freeware metrics, blog/social media content, and time stamps can provide valuable insight into an individual's working process and differentiate learners in a network.

In the larger scheme of things, Peeragogical assessment provides direct access to and practice in the culture learners will be expected to join when they complete their course of study. Collaboration, delegation, facilitating conversations, and other highly valued skills are developed in plain view, where progress can be critiqued and validated by peers, experts and the public.

But tall trees don't grow by themselves in the desert. Peeragogical innovation can be challenging in organizational cultures that prioritize control and standardization; as Senge *et al.* have observed, the system doesn't evaluate quality when dealing with the unfamiliar, it just pushes back. In schools this is so typical that it doesn't merit comment in traditional media. The world notices when Syria goes dark, but in school, restricted online access is business as usual.

Cultural constraints can make early adopters in technology-based Peeragogy seem like Promethean risk-takers. Whenever the author gives a talk or an interview, someone asks if he's in trouble.

Learners are not fooled by the rhetoric of in loco parentis or vision statements that emphasize "safe, nurturing learning environments." With notable exceptions, today's school leaders do not know as much about technology as the young people for whom they assume responsibility. Still, learners understand survival: they are fighting in unfavorable terrain against an enemy of great power. Innovating is impossible, and even loudly criticizing school or advocating for change is a risk. As a result many do just enough to satisfy requirements without getting involved enough to attract attention. Some have also internalized the critical voices of authority or the failure of the formal experience as evidence of their own inability: "I'm just not good at math."

How do we know when we're really good at something? Standardized testing feedback doesn't help learners improve. Most of us don't have a natural talent for offering or accepting criticism. And yet, as Wole Soyinka put it, "The greatest threat to freedom is the absence of criticism." Peeragogical interaction requires refining relational and topical critique, as well as skills in other "meta" literacies, including but not limited to critical thinking, collaboration, conflict resolution, decision-making, mindfulness, patience and compassion.

Interpersonal learning skills are undervalued in today's schooling paradigm. Consequently there is an operational lack of incentive for teachers and learners to devote time and energy, particularly when it carries a perceived cost in achievement on tests that determine financial allocations and job security. In recent years there has been increasing pressure to tie teacher compensation, performance evaluation, and job status directly to student performance on standardized tests.

Some educators are introducing peer-to-peer network language and even introducing peer-based assessment. But the contracts, syllabi and letters to students typically stink of *the old way*. These one-to-many documents are presented by agents of the institution endowed with the power to reward or punish. To many students this does not represent a choice or a real opportunity to hack the learning experience. They suspect manipulation, and they wait for the other shoe to drop. Learners also don't like to be told they're free while being forced to operate within tight constraints. Consider this likely reaction to a policy that is highly regarded in the field:

> "Students may choose to reblog their work in a public place or on their own blogs, but do so at their own risk."
>
> *(What? Did I read that correctly?)*
>
> "Students may choose to reblog their work in a public place or on their own blogs, but do so at their own risk."
>
> *(Risk? What risk? The risk of possibly helping someone understand something that they didn't before, or get a different opinion than the one they had before? Someone please help me make sense of this.)*

To effectively adopt Peeragogical assessment in the schooling context, the community must construct a new understanding of how the members in a network relate to one another independent of their roles in the surrounding social or hierarchical systems. This requires trust, which in school requires significant suspension of disbelief, which – and this is the hard part – requires actual substantive, structural change in the learning transaction. This is the defining characteristic of Open Source Learning: as the network grows, changes composition, and changes purpose, it also changes the direction and content of the learning experience. Every network member can introduce new ideas, ask questions, and contribute resources than refine and redirect the process.

This isn't easy. A member in this network must forget what she knows about school in order to test the boundaries of learning that shape her relationship to content, peers, and expert sources of information and feedback. This is how the cogs in the machine become the liminal heroes who redesign it. Having rejected the old way, they must now create the rituals that will come to define the new. They are following in the path of Oedipus, who took on the inscrutable and intimidating Sphinx, solved the riddle that had killed others who tried, and ushered out the old belief systems to pave the way for the Gods of Olympus. Imagine what would have happened if Oedipus had had the Internet.

# Part III

# Peeragogy in Practice

CHAPTER 5

# THINKING ABOUT PATTERNS

> Although a grounding in learning theory helps inform peer learning projects, Peeragogy, at its core, comes to life in applied practice. Even before convening a group for your peer learning project (discussed in Part IV), you will want to take a look over the patterns we have collected. You will likely return here many times as your project develops.

## What is a pattern?

A pattern is anything that has a repeated effect. In the context of peeragogy, the practice is to repeat processes and interactions that advance the learning mission. Frequent occurrences that are not desirable are called anti-patterns!

> **Christopher Alexander**: "Each pattern describes a problem which occurs over and over again in our environment, and then describes the core of the solution to that problem, in a way that you can use this solution a million times over, without ever doing it the same way twice." [1]

Patterns provide a framework that can be applied to similar issues but may be metaphorically solved in different ways, sometimes in real world or face to face events and other times in digital space. Outside of Alexander's own work in architecture, one the first groups to adopt a design pattern way of thinking about things were computer programmers. Writing in the foreward to Richard P. Gabriel's *Patterns of Software*, Alexander emphasizes that the key question to ask about any design approach is: does it help us build better?

> **Christopher Alexander**: "What is the Chartres of programming? What task is at a high enough level to inspire people writing programs, to reach for the stars?" [2]

We think that Peeragogy stands a good chance of being a "killer app" for pattern-based design. Learning bridges physical and virtual worlds all the time. And, in fact, a *Network of Learning* was the 18th pattern that Christopher Alexander introduced in his book, *A Pattern Language.*

> **Christopher Alexander**: "Work in piecemeal ways to decentralize the process of learning and enrich it through contact with many places and people all over the city: workshops, teachers at home or walking through the city, professionals willing to take on the young as helpers, older children teaching younger children, museums, youth groups travelling, scholarly seminars, industrial workshops, old people, and so on." [1]

Peeragogy can help to extend and enrich this network, and, as we shall see, patterns can be used by those involved to do ongoing "emergent" design, not only by building new structures, but by adapting and improving our catalog of patterns as we go. For consistency, and easy use, adaptation, and extension we present the patterns using the following template. The format is meant to be neutral and easy to work with – it's, intentionally, an outline that you might use to write a short abstract describing an active project.

> **Title**: *Encapsulate the idea - possibly include a subtitle*
>
> **Context**: *Describe the context in which it is meaningful. What are the key **forces** acting in this context?*
>
> **Problem**: *Explain why there's some issue to address here.*

**Solution**: *Talk about an idea about how to address the issue.*

**Rationale**: *Why do we use this solution as opposed to some other solution?*

**Resolution**: *How are the key forces resolved when the solution is applied?*

**What's Next**: *Talk about specific next steps. How will the active forces continue to resolve in our project?*

Patterns optionally include the following optional elements:

[**Examples**: *Present example(s) that have been encountered, if this aids comprehension.*]

[**References**: *Citations, if relevant.*]

The "What's Next" section concretely links the patterns we discuss here to the Peeragogy project. It can be thought of as an annotation rather than part of the pattern itself. If you adapt the patterns for use in your own project, you're likely to have a different set of next steps. Although we think that these patterns can be generally useful, they aren't useful in the abstract, but rather, as a way for discussing what we actually do.

## A peeragogy pattern language

By looking at how patterns combine in real and hypothetical use cases, you can start to identify a *pattern language* that can be used in your projects. We can get a simplified view of these connections with the following diagram. It's important to clarify that everyone doesn't do it the same way. Here, the *Roadmap* is given a central position, but some peer learning projects will forego making a specific, detailed plan; their plan is just to see what develops. You can see here how peeragogy patterns often break down further into individual micro-steps: we'll say more about that shortly.

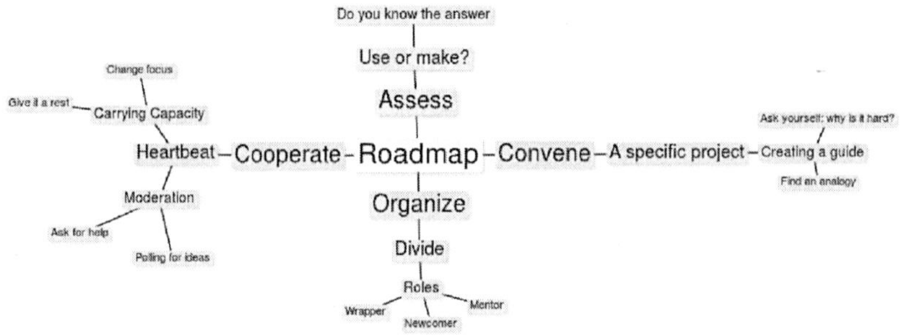


The subsequent main sections of this book – *Convene*, *Organize*, *Cooperate* and *Assess* (for short) – represent big clusters of patterns that are likely to come up time and again in various projects. We can think of these as East, South, West, and North in the diagram above. You are encouraged to invent your own patterns and to connect them in new ways. You'll probably find quite a few that we didn't include in the catalog. Each project has a unique design, and it's own unique way in which things play out in practice. What we've put together here is a starter kit. The peeragogy patterns suggest a social way to do problem solving [3], but once you get used to the pattern concept you can use it to identify new problems no one has ever thought of before, and that's even more powerful!

## References

1. Alexander, C., Ishikawa, S., and Silverstein, M. (1977). *A Pattern Language: Towns, Buildings, and, Construction*, New York: Oxford University Press.
2. Gabriel, Richard P. (1996). *Patterns of Software*, New York: Oxford University Press. (Includes a foreward by Christopher Alexander.)
3. Minsky, Marvin. (2008–2009). *Essays on Education (for OLPC)*, Massachusetts Institute of Technology Media Lab whitepaper, Available online.

CHAPTER 6

# PATTERNS OF PEERAGOGY

Readers will have encountered *peer production*, at least in applications like Wikipedia, StackExchange, and free/libre/open source software development. Readers will also be familiar with *peeragogy*, even if the name is unfamiliar. Simply put, peeragogy is active learning together with others. Participants in a peeragogical endeavor collaboratively build emergent structures that are responsive to their changing context. They learn – and they adapt. Taking inspiration from the notable successes of peer production, we are using peeragogy to help design the future of learning, inside and outside of institutions.

We have found design patterns useful for organizing our work on this momentous task. However, there is a difference between the pattern language we present here and previous collections of design patterns that touch on similar domains – like *Liberating Voices: A Pattern Language for Communication Revolution* [11] and *Pedagogical Patterns: Advice for Educators* [3]. At the level of the pattern template, our innovation is simply to add a "What's next" annotation to each pattern, which anticipates the way the pattern will continue to "resolve" in our work.

This mirrors the central considerations of our approach, which is all about human interaction, and the challenges, fluidity and lack of predictability that comes with it. Something that works for one person may not work for another or may not even work for the same person in a slightly different situation. Nevertheless, it is hard to argue with a formula like "If W applies, do X to get Y." In our view, other pattern languages often achieve this sort of common sense rationality, and then stop. Failure in the prescriptive model only begins when people try to define things more carefully and make context-specific changes – when they actually try to put ideas into practice. The problem lies in the inevitable distance between *do as I say*, *do as I do*, and *do with me*

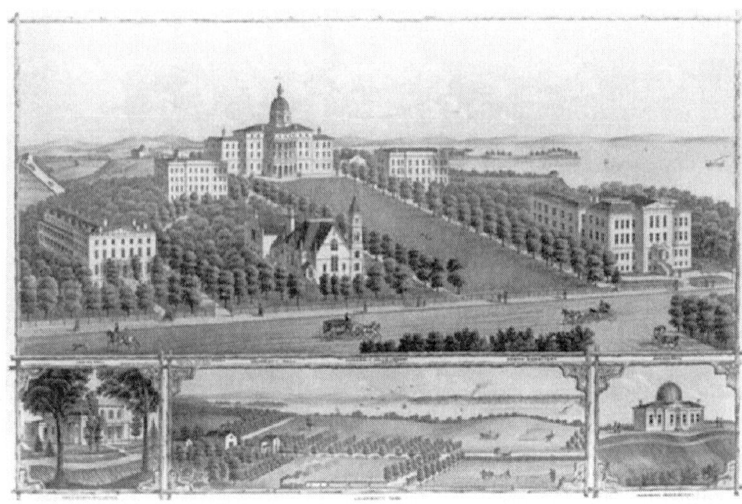

Figure 6.1: A prototypical university. Caption reads: "Wisconsin State University, Madison, Wis. 1879". Inset captions describe the pictured buildings: "Ladies Hall, South Dormitory, University Hall, Assembly Halls & Library, North Dormitory, Science Hall, President's Residence, University Farm, and Washburn Observatory." Public domain.

[7, p. 26].

This paper outlines a new approach to the organization of learning, drawing on the principles of free/libre/open source software (FLOSS) and open culture. Mako Hill suggests that one recipe for success in peer production is to take a familiar idea – his example is an encyclopedia – and make it easy for people to participate in building it [9, Chapter 1]. Another inspiring familiar idea is the university. We will take hold of "learning in institutions" as a map (Figure 6.1), though it does not fully conform to the tacitly-familiar territory of peeragogy. To be clear, peeragogy is not just for teachers and students, but for *any group of people who want to learn anything.*

Indeed, the strong version of our claim is that peeragogy is needed in applications of any map, blueprint, or design that seeks to involve people as people. In some idealized sense, "control" is all that's required to move from a well-thought-out design to successful execution. But, at the very least, this leaves the question: where do the designs come from in the first place [12]? Once they exist, designs need to be interpreted, and often, revised. People may think that they are on the same page, only to find out that their understandings are wildly different. For example, everyone may agree that the group needs to go "that way." But how far? How fast? It is rare for a project to be able to set or even define all parameters accurately and concisely at the beginning.

This is true for pattern languages as well. We describe them in text, but they become a "living language" [1, p. xvii] just insofar as they are linked to action. Many things have changed since Alexander suggested that "you will get the most 'power' over the language, and make it your own most effectively, if you write the changes in, at the appropriate places in the book" [1, p. xl]. We see more clearly that we can build living designs, and inscribe their changing form not just in the margins of a book, or even a shared wiki, but in the lifeworld itself.

Although we are often thinking about learning and adaptation that takes place far outside of formal institutions, the historical conception of the university can offer some guidance. The model university is not separate from the life of the state or its citizenry, but aims to "assume leadership in the application of knowledge for the direct improvement of the life of the people in every sphere" [6, p. 88]. Research that *adds to the store of knowledge* is another fundamental obligation [6, p. 550].

Our emergent approach to collaboration and knowledge-building is likely to be of interest to theorists in fields like organization studies and, perhaps surprisingly, computer science, where researchers are increasingly making use of social approaches to software design and development (e.g., via the Manifesto for Agile Software Development) as well as agent-based models of computation and learning [10, 5]. The design pattern community in particular is very familiar with practices that we think of as peeragogical, notably shepherding and writers workshops [8, 4]. We hope to help design pattern authors and researchers expand on these strengths.

The next section introduces PEERAGOGY more explicitly in the form of a design pattern. Sections 6–6 present the other patterns in our pattern language. Figure 6.2 illustrates their interconnections. In each pattern description, the key forces that apply within the pattern's context are highlighted in bold face. Each pattern also includes two examples. The first example shows how the pattern is exhibited in current Wikimedia projects. We have selected Wikimedia as a source of examples because we are relatively familiar with it, and because the relevant data is readily available to readers. The second example shows how the given pattern could be applied in the design of a future university. Whereas existing projects like Wikimedia's Wikiversity and the Peer-2-Peer University (P2PU) have created "a model for lifelong learning alongside traditional formal higher education," they stop well short of offering accredited degrees. What would an accredited free/libre/open university offering general education look like? How would it compare or contrast with the typical or stereotypical image of a university from Figure 6.1?

Each pattern concludes with a "What's next" annotation, and Chapter 7 collects these next steps and summarizes the outlook of the Peeragogy project. It also sums up what's unique about this catalog, positioning it work as a hands-on complement to existing sociological and historical research about peer production (surveyed in [2]).

## References

1. Christopher Alexander, Sara Ishikawa, and Murray Silverstein. *A Pattern Language: Towns, Buildings, Construction.* Center for Environmental Structure Series. Oxford: Oxford University Press, 1977.
2. Yochai Benkler, Aaron Shaw, and Benjamin Mako Hill. "Peer production: a modality of collective intelligence". In: *The Collective Intelligence Handbook.* Ed. by Thomas W. Malone and Michael S. Bernstein. To appear. MIT Press, 2015.

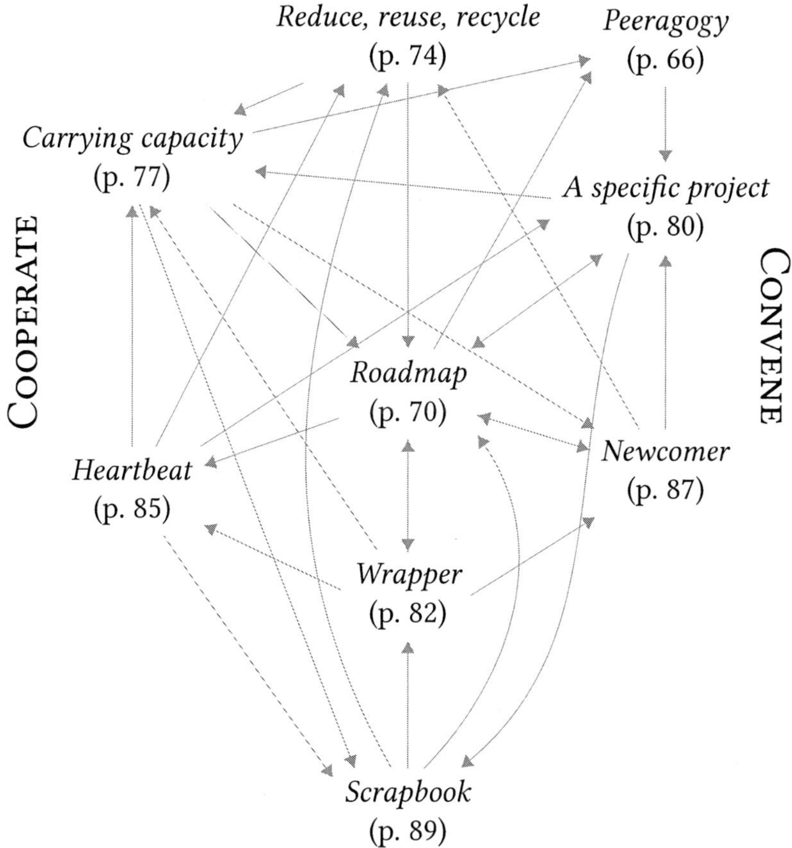


Figure 6.2: Connections between the patterns of peeragogy. An arrow points from pattern **A** to pattern **B** if the description of pattern **A** references pattern **B**. Labels at the borders of the figure correspond to the main sections of the *Peeragogy Handbook.*

3. Joseph Bergin et al. *Pedagogical patterns: Advice for educators.* New York: Joseph Bergin Software Tools, 2012.
4. James O Coplien and B Woolf. "A pattern language for writers' workshops". In: *C++ report* 9 (1997), pp. 51–60.
5. J. Corneli et al. "Computational Poetry Workshop: Making Sense of Work in Progress". In: *Proceedings of the Sixth International Conference on Computational Creativity, ICCC 2015.* Ed. by Simon Colton et al. 2015. URL: http://metameso.org/~joe/docs/poetryICCC-wip.pdf.
6. Merle Eugene Curti et al. *The University of Wisconsin, a history: 1848-1925.* Univ. of Wisconsin Press, 1949.
7. Gilles Deleuze. *Difference and repetition.* London: Bloomsbury Academic, 2004.
8. Neil B Harrison. "The Language of Shepherding". In: *Pattern Languages of Program Design* 5 (1999), pp. 507–530.
9. Benjamin Mako Hill. "Essays on Volunteer Mobilization in Peer Production". PhD thesis. Massachusetts Institute of Technology, 2013. URL: http://dspace.mit.edu/handle/1721.1/86240.
10. Marvin Minsky. "Why programming is a good medium for expressing poorly understood and sloppily formulated ideas". In: *Design and Planning II-Computers in Design and Communication.* Visual Committee Books. 1967, pp. 120–125.
11. Douglas Schuler. *Liberating voices: A pattern language for communication revolution.* Cambridge, MA: MIT Press, 2008.
12. Heinz Von Foerster. "Cybernetics of cybernetics". In: *Understanding Understanding.* Springer, 2003 [1979], pp. 283–286.

## Peeragogy

**Context** Architectual maverick Christopher Alexander [1] asked the following questions to an audience of computer programmers:

> "What is the Chartres of programming? What task is at a high enough level to inspire people writing programs, to reach for the stars?"

In order for humanity to pull itself up by its bootstraps, on this planet or any other, we need to continue to learn and adapt. Collaborative projects like Wikipedia, StackExchange, and FLOSS represent an implicit challenge to the old "industrial" organization of work. This new way of working appears to promise something more resilient, more exciting, and more humane. In the context of these free, open, post-modern organizations, individual participants are learning and growing – and adapting the methods and infrastructure as they go. Because everyone in these projects primarily learns by putting in effort on a shared work-in-progress, participants are more in touch with an *equality of intelligence* than an *inequality of knowledge* [4, pp. 38,119]. At the same time, they invoke a form of friendly competition, in which *the best craftmanship wins* [5, p. 89]. **There is a tension between the inclusiveness of an "open" work and the specificity required in order to develop something really useful. The trust that is required to sustain a culture of learning is only built through sharing and reciprocity.**

**Problem** Even a highly successful project like Wikipedia is a work in progress that can be improved to better *empower and engage people around the world, to develop* richer and more useful *educational content, and to disseminate it* more *effectively* – and deploy it more creatively. How to go about this is a difficult question, and we don't know the answers in advance. There are rigorous challenges facing smaller projects as well, and fewer resources to draw on. Many successful free software projects are not particularly collaborative – and the largest projects are edited only by a small minority of users [3, 8]. Can we work smarter together?

**Solution** People who learn actively together talk to each other about material problems, share practical solutions, and constructively critique works-in-progress. There are many different ways to go about this – bug reports, mailing lists, writers workshops, Q&A forums, watercoolers and skateparks are all places where peeragogy can happen. We have found that the necessary "reflection" aspects of the process are particularly well-matched to Christopher Alexander's idea of a *pattern language*, in which commonly occurring, interconnected, elements of an optative design are refined until they can be described in terms of a simple template. Indeed, thought of as a design pattern, PEERAGOGY can be understood as an up-to-date revision of Alexander's NETWORK OF LEARNING [2, p. 99]. It *decentralizes the process of learning and enriches it through contact with many places and people* – in interconnected networks that may reach all over the world. Importantly, while people involved in a peeragogical process may be collaborating on A SPECIFIC PROJECT, they don't have to be direct collaborators outside of the learning context or co-located in time or space. Peeragogy often takes place in mostly-horizontal relationships between people who have different but compatible objectives.

**Rationale** The peeragogical approach particularly addresses the problems of small projects stuck in their individual silos, and large projects becoming overwhelmed by their own complexity. It does this by going the opposite route: explicating *what by definition is tacit* and employing *a continuous design process* [6, pp. 9–10]. The very act of asking "can we work smarter together?" puts learning front and center. PEERAGOGY takes that "center" and distributes it across a pool of heterogeneous relationships. As pedagogy articulates the transmission of knowledge from teachers to students, peeragogy articulates the way peers produce and use knowledge together (Figure 6.2). Active learning together with others brings social and emotional intelligence to bear on the things that matter most.

**Resolution** Peeragogy helps people in different projects describe and solve real problems. If you share the problems that you're experiencing in your project, someone may be able to help you solve them. This process can guide individual action in ways that we wouldn't have seen on our own, and may lead to new forms of collective action we would never have imagined possible. Making room for multiple right answers resolves the tension between generality and specificity. The Peeragogy project is one of "tens of thousands of projects in the traditions of world improvement élan – without any central committee that would have to, or even could, tell the active what their next operations should be" [7, p. 402]. When we talk about "next steps," we aim to clarify our own commitments, and show what can be realistically expected from us.

**Example 1** Wikipedia and its sister sites rely on user generated content, peer produced software, and are managed, by and large, by a pool of users who choose to get involved with governance and other "meta" duties. Wikimedia's pluralistic approach achieves something quite impressive: the Wikimedia Foundation runs the 7$^{th}$ most popular website in the world, and has around 230 employees. For comparison, the 6$^{th}$ and 8$^{th}$ most popular websites are run by companies with 150K and 30K employees, respectively.

**Example 2** Although one of the strengths of PEERAGOGY is to distribute the workload, this does not mean that infrastructure is irrelevant. No less than their predecessors, the students and researchers of the future university will need access to an Observatory and other scientific apparatus if they are truly to reach *ad astra, per aspera.*

> *What's next.* We intend to revise and extend the patterns and methods of peeragogy to make it a workable model for learning, inside or outside of institutions.

### References

1. Christopher Alexander. “The origins of pattern theory: The future of the theory, and the generation of a living world”. In: *Software, IEEE* 16.5 (1999), pp. 71–82.
2. Christopher Alexander, Sara Ishikawa, and Murray Silverstein. *A Pattern Language: Towns, Buildings, Construction.* Center for Environmental Structure Series. Oxford: Oxford University Press, 1977.
3. Benjamin Mako Hill. *When Free Software Isn't (Practically) Better.* Published on gnu.org. Licensed via CC-By-SA. 2011. URL: `http://www.gnu.org/philosophy/when_free_software_isnt_practically_better.html`.
4. Jacques Rancière. *The ignorant schoolmaster: Five lessons in intellectual emancipation.* Stanford University Press, 1991 [1987].
5. Eric S Raymond. *The Cathedral & the Bazaar: Musings on Linux and open source by an accidental revolutionary.* O'Reilly Media, Inc., 2001.
6. Till Schümmer, Joerg M Haake, and Wolfgang Stark. “Beyond rational design patterns”. In: *Proceedings of the 19th European Conference on Pattern Languages of Programs.* ACM. 2014, 13 pp.
7. P. Sloterdijk. *You Must Change Your Life.* Polity Press, 2013.
8. Aaron Swartz. *Who Writes Wikipedia?* Published on aaronsw.com. 2006. URL: `http://www.aaronsw.com/weblog/whowriteswikipedia`.

## Roadmap

**Context** PEERAGOGY has both distributed and centralized aspects. The different discussants or contributors who collaborate on a project have different points of view and heterogeneous priorities, but they come together in conversations and joint activities. **Different people will have different goals and interests in mind; some may be quite specific, and some rather vague. Upon further scrutiny, some of these goals will be seen to be well-aligned, others less so.**

**Problem** In order to collaborate, people need a way to share current, though incomplete, understanding of the space they are working in, and to nurture relationships with one another and the other elements of this space. Without a sense of our individual goals or how they fit together in the context of addressing outstanding problems, it is difficult for people to help out, or to assess the project's progress. At the outset, there may not even be a project or a vision for a project, but a only loose collection of motivations and sentiments. Once the project is running, people are likely to pull in different directions.

**Solution** Building a guide to current and upcoming activities, experiments, goals and working methods can help NEWCOMERS and old-timers alike see where they can jump in. This guide may take various forms, and different levels of detail. It may be a research question or an outline, an organizational mission statement or a business plan. It may be a design pattern or a pattern language [3]. It may combine features of a manifesto, a syllabus, and an issue tracker. The distinguishing qualities of a project ROADMAP are that it should be adaptive to circumstances and that it should ultimately get us from *here* to *there*. By this same token, any given version of the roadmap is seen as fallible. It should be accessible to everyone with an interest in the project, though in practice not everyone will choose to update it. In lieu of widespread participation, the project's WRAPPER should attempt to synthesize an accurate roadmap informed by participants' behavior, and should help moderate in case of conflict. However, full consensus is not necessary. Different goals, with different *heres* and *theres*, can be pursued separately, while maintaining communication. To the extent that it's possible, combining everyone's individual plan into an overall ROADMAP can help give everyone a sense of what's going on.

**Rationale** Unless the project's plan is easy for people to see and to update, they are not likely to use it, and are less likely to get involved. The key point of the roadmap is to help support involvement by those who *are* involved. The level of detail in the roadmap (and the existence of a roadmap at all) should correspond to the felt need for sharing information and to the tolerance of uncertainty among participants. The structure of the roadmap should be able shift along with its contents: it is an antidote to TUNNEL VISION [1, pp. 121–124]. In the Peeragogy project our roadmap evolved from an outline of the first draft of the *Peeragogy Handbook*, to a schedule of meetings with a regular "HEARTBEAT" supplemented by a list of upcoming submission deadlines, to the emergent objectives listed in Section 7 of the current paper. By contrast, we've seen that a list of nice-to-have features is comparatively unlikely to *go* anywhere. A backlog of tasks and a realistic plan for accomplishing them can be vastly different things. An adaptive roadmap that incorporates multiple simultaneous solution paths can achieve integration around core values without over-determining or over-constraining participation.

**Resolution** Using the pattern catalog as an organizational tool gives us a robust mechanism for building and maintaining a "distributed", and ultimately "emergent" roadmap – whose components are rooted in real problems and justifiable solutions, with a concrete resolution and followthrough. When these components are put together, we get a reasonably coherent and actionable idea of where the project is going. The roadmap can give NEWCOMERS a reasonable idea of what it would mean to participate in the project, and can help them decide whether, where, and how to get involved.

**Example 1** The *Help* link present on every Wikipedia page could be seen as a localized ROADMAP for individual user engagement. It tells users what they can do on the site:

> I want to read or find an article; I want to edit an article; I want to report a problem with an article; I want to create a new article or upload media; I have a factual question... [Etc.]

Community-organized WikiProjects and official Wikimedia projects announce their objectives and invite others to get involved (cf. A SPECIFIC PROJECT). Wikimedia previously developed a detailed strategic plan drawing on community input [2]. The current description of the State of the Wikimedia Foundation includes a pointer to a two-week 2015 Strategy Community Consultation (now closed for purposes of review and synthesis)."

**Example 2** In the future university, maintaining a special President's Residence would presumably be an undue opulence. However it may be appropriate for project facilitators to gather at a University Hall for the primary purpose of working together on the university's ROADMAP. For now, we mostly meet online, and in person less frequently: at cafes, when passing through town, or at conferences. In New York alone, there are a million members of meetup.com with similar habits, although they most likely have never heard of peeragogy. There is strength in numbers – and there is leverage in organization. Whatever we balance we strike between "global" and "local" operations, the purpose of our roadmap is to help us get organized.

*What's Next.* If we sense that something needs to change about the project, that is a clue that we might need to record a new pattern, or revise our existing patterns.

## References

1. David M. Dikel, David Kane, and James R. Wilson. *Software architecture: Organizational Principles and Patterns.* Pearson Education, 2001.

2. Eugene Eric Kim et al. *Wikimedia Strategic Plan: A collaborative vision for the movement through 2015*. Wikimedia Foundation, 2011.

3. Christian Kohls. "The structure of patterns". In: *Proceedings of the 17th Conference on Pattern Languages of Programs*. ACM. 2010, p. 12.

## Reduce, reuse, recycle

**Context** In a peer production context, you are simultaneously "making stuff" and building on the work of others. **You don't have to do everything yourself! The library of resources you can draw on is vast – but it is useful only if you can make sense of it.**

**Problem** People are often very attached to their own projects and priorities and don't have a sense of how their initiatives can benefit from connection and relationship. Many projects die because the cost of REINVENTING THE WHEEL [c2] is too high.

**Solution** "Steal like an artist," and make it possible for other people to build on your work too (Figure 6.3). In the Peeragogy project, we have written very little new software, and have instead used off-the-shelf and hosted solutions suited to the task at hand (including: Drupal, Google+, Google Hangouts, Google Docs, Wordpress, pandoc, XeLaTeX, Authorea, and Github). Early on we agreed to release our *Peeragogy Handbook* under the terms of the Creative Commons Public Domain Dedication (CC0), the legal instrument that grants the greatest possible leeway to downstream users. This has allowed us and others to repurpose and improve its contents in other settings, including the current paper. In short, follow the steps indicated by the keywords in the pattern's title: *Reduce* the panoply of interesting interrelated ideas and methods to a functional core (e.g. writing a book). *Reuse* whatever resources are relevant to this aim, factoring in "things I

Figure 6.3: A paradigmatic example of found-art. Caption reads: "Fountain by R. Mutt, Photograph by Alfred Stieglitz, THE EXHIBIT REFUSED BY THE INDEPENDENTS". Public domain, via the Wikimedia Commons.

was going to have to do anyway" from everyone involved. *Recycle* what you've created in new connections and relationships.

**Rationale** Clearly we are not the first people to notice the problems with wheel-reinvention, including "missing opportunities, repeating common mistakes, and working harder than we need to." As a guest in one of our hangouts, Willow Brugh, of Geeks without Bounds and the MIT Media Lab, remarked that *people often think that they need to build a community, and so fail to recognize that they are already part of a community.*

**Resolution** Peeragogy per se is not new, and it's not something we can bottle and sell. It appears in avocational, academic, and industrial contexts. We can, however, learn how to be more capable peeragogues with practice. Reweaving old material into new designs and new material into existing frameworks, we build deeper understanding. The project's ROADMAP develops by making sense of existing resources – including worries and concerns. This boosts our collective CARRYING CAPACITY.

**Example 1** Users are encouraged to recycle existing works that are compatible with the Wikimedia-wide CC-By-SA license, and the mission of the respective sites (e.g. books on Wikibooks or Wikisource, dictionary entries on Wiktionary, encyclopedic writing on Wikipedia, etc.). Subprojects have existed purely to help repurpose other existing works in this way. On the downstream side, DBPedia is an important resource for the semantic web, built by collating data from Wikipedia's "infoboxes". Researchers have been able to REDUCE, REUSE, RECYCLE in other ways, e.g. by developing tools for building learning paths through Wikipedia content, or that show heatmaps of editing activity. However, these research projects do not always result in a tool that is accessible to day-to-day users.

**Example 2** The knowledge resources and collaboration tools currently available online are what make a low-cost, high-quality, formally-accredited future university conceivable. However, the available resources are not always as organized as they would need to be for educative purposes, so peeragogues can usefully put effort into REDUCE, REUSE, RECYCLE'ing available resources into a functioning university Library.

> *What's Next.* We've converted our old pattern catalog from the *Peeragogy Handbook* into this paper, sharing it with a new community and gaining new perspectives. Can we repeat that for other things we've made?

# Carrying Capacity

**Context** One of the important maxims from the world of FLOSS is: "Given enough eyeballs, all bugs are shallow" [6, p. 30]. A partial converse is also true. **There's only so much any one person can do with limited resources and a limited amount of time. Furthermore, in a peeragogy context, it is often impossible to delegate work to others. Lines of responsibility are not always clear, and people can easily get burnt out. Our concern is not simply "inclusion" but rather to help everyone involved fulfil their potential. This will not happen for someone who takes on too much, or someone who takes on too little.**

**Problem** How can we help prevent those people who are involved with the project from overpromising or overcommitting, and subsequently crashing and burning? First, let's be clear that are lots of ways things can go wrong. Simplistic expectations – like *assuming that others will do the work for you* [9] – can undermine your ability to correctly gauge your own strengths, weaknesses, and commitments. Without careful, critical engagement, you might not even notice when there's a problem. Where one person has trouble letting go, others may have trouble speaking up. Pressure builds when communication isn't going well.

**Solution** Symptoms of burnout are a sign that it's time to revisit the group's ROADMAP and your own individual plan. Are these realistic? Frustration with other people is a good time to ask questions and let others answer. Do they see things the same way you do? Your goals may be aligned, even if your methods and motivations differ. If you have a "buddy" they can provide a reality check. Maybe things are not *that hard* after all – and maybe they don't need to be done *right now*. Generalizing from this: the project can promote an open dialog by creating opportunities for people to share their worries and generate an emergent plan for addressing them [8]. Use the project SCRAPBOOK to make note of obstacles. For example, if you'd like to pass a baton, you'll need someone there who can take it. Maybe you can't find that person right away, but you can bring up the concern and get it onto the project's ROADMAP. The situation is always changing, but if we continue to create suitable checkpoints and benchmarks, then we can take steps to take care of an issue that's getting bogged down.

**Rationale** Think of the project as an ecosystem populated by acts of participation. As we get to know more about ourselves and each other, we know what sorts of things we can expect, and we are able to work together more sustainably [4]. We can regulate our individual stress levels and improve collective outcomes by discussing concerns openly.

**Resolution** Guiding and rebalancing behaviour in a social context may begin by simply speaking up about a concern. What we learn in this process is consistent with inclusivity [1], but goes further, as participants are invited to be candid about what works well for them and what does not. As we share concerns and are met with care and practical support, our actions begin to align better with expectations (often as a result of forming more realistic expectations). When we have the opportunity to express and rethink our concerns, we can become more clear about the commitments we're prepared to make. As we become aware of the problems others are facing, we often find places where we ourselves have something to learn.

**Example 1** Wikipedia aims to emphasize a neutral point of view, but its users are not neutral. Wikipedia is relevant to things that matter to us. It helps inform us regarding our necessary purposes – and we are invited to "speak up" by making edits on pages that matter to us. However, coverage and participation are not neutral in another sense. More information on Wikipedia deals with Europe than all of the locations outside of Europe [3]. A recent solicitation for donations to the Wikimedia Foundation says "Wikipedia has over 450 million readers. Less than 1% give." As we remarked in the PEERAGOGY pattern, most of the actual work is contibuted by a small percentage of users as well. Furthermore, the technology limits what can be said; [3] remark on "the structural inability of the platform itself to incorporate fundamental epistemological diversity." Finally, the overall population of editors is an important concern for the Wikimedia Foundation: the total number of active editors has been falling since 2007.

**Example 2** A separate Ladies Hall seems entirely archaic. Progressive thinkers have for some time subscribed to the view that "there shall be no women in case there be not men, nor men in case there be not women" [5, Chapter 1.LII]. However, in light of the extreme gender imbalance in free software, and still striking imbalance at Wikipedia [2, 7], it will be important to do whatever it takes to make women and girls welcome, not least because this is a significant factor in boosting our CARRYING CAPACITY.

*What's Next.* Making it easy and fruitful for others to get involved is one of the best ways to redistribute the load. This often requires skill development among those involved; compare the NEWCOMER pattern.

## References


1. D Randy Garrison and Zehra Akyol. "Toward the development of a metacognition construct for communities of inquiry". In: *The Internet and Higher Education* 17 (2013), pp. 84–89.
2. Rishab A. Ghosh et al. *Free/Libre and Open Source Software: Survey and Study.* Tech. rep. D18. International Institute of Infonomics, University of Maastricht, 2002.
3. Mark Graham et al. "Uneven geographies of user-generated information: patterns of increasing informational poverty". In: *Annals of the Association of American Geographers* 104.4 (2014), pp. 746–764.

4. Elinor Ostrom. "Revising theory in light of experimental findings". In: *Journal of Economic Behavior & Organization* 73.1 (2010), pp. 68–72.
5. François Rabelais. *Gargantua and Pantagruel.* Moray Press, 1894.
6. Eric S Raymond. *The Cathedral & the Bazaar: Musings on Linux and open source by an accidental revolutionary.* O'Reilly Media, Inc., 2001.
7. Joseph Reagle. ""Free as in sexist?" Free culture and the gender gap". In: *First Monday* 18.1 (2012). ISSN: 13960466. URL: `http://firstmonday.org/ojs/index.php/fm/article/view/4291`.
8. Jaakko Seikkula and Tom Erik Arnkil. *Dialogical meetings in social networks.* Karnac Books, 2006.
9. Linus Torvalds and Steven Vaughan-Nichols. *Linus Torvalds's Lessons on Software Development Management.* 2011. URL: `http://web.archive.org/web/20131021211847/http://h30565.www3.hp.com/t5/Feature-Articles/Linus-Torvalds-s-Lessons-on-Software-Development-Management/ba-p/440`.


## A specific project

**Context** We often find ourselves confronted with what seems to be a difficult, complex, or even insurmountable problem. It won't go away, but a workable solution doesn't present itself, either. If there is a candidate solution, it's also clear there are not enough resources for it to be feasible. **In the face of serious difficulties we often find ourselves wringing our hands, or preaching to the choir about things they already know. It is harder to make actionable plans and follow them through to bring about concrete change.**

**Problem** We are often blinded by our own prejudices and preferences. Considerable energy goes into pondering, discussing, exploring and feeling stuck. Meanwhile there may be a strong urge to make more concrete progress, and time is passing by. In a group setting, when the forward-movers ultimately try to act, those who are more wrapped up in the experience of pondering and exploring may attempt to shut them down, if they feel that they are being left behind. Inaction may seem like the only safe choice, but it has risks too.

**Solution** One of the best ways to start to make concrete progress on a hard problem is to ask a specific question. Formulating a question helps your thinking become more concrete. Sometimes you'll see that a solution was within your grasp all along, and you don't actually need to ask the question to anyone anymore. In the case of a truly difficult problem, one question won't be enough, but you can repeat the process: turning something that is too large or too ephemeral to tackle directly into a collection of smaller, specific, manageable tasks that you can learn something from. Maintain an overall project Roadmap to keep track of how the smaller pieces relate to the bigger picture. If you have a fairly specific idea about what you want to do, but you're finding it difficult to get it done, don't just ask for advice: recruit material help (cf. Carrying capacity).

**Rationale** We've seen time and again that asking specific questions is a recipe for getting concrete, and that getting concrete is necessary for bringing about change. Asking for help (which is what happens when you vocalize a question) is one of the best ways to gain coherence. Making yourself understood can go a long way toward resolving deeper difficulties.

**Resolution** Where you may have felt stuck or realized you were going in circles, getting specific allows forward progress. The struggle between consensus and action is resolved in a tangible project that combines action with dialog. Learning something new is a strong sign that things are working. Real change starts out "bite-sized."

**Example 1** One of the best ways to jump in, get to know other Wikipedia users, and start working on a focused todo list is to join (or start) A SPECIFIC PROJECT. Within Wikipedia, these are known as "WikiProjects." The Wikimedia Foundation also runs public projects, including the Wikipedia Education Program and the GLAM Wiki (for Galleries, Libraries, Archives, and Museums). The latter maintains a *list of case studies that describes specific projects undertaken by cultural organizations and Wikimedia.*

**Example 2** Dormitories could be seen as an "optional extra," since studying from where you live is often an option already. However, rented or cooperatively-owned living/working spaces may frequently be an asset for A SPECIFIC PROJECT.

*What's Next.* We need to build specific, tangible "what's next" steps and connect them with concrete action. Use the SCRAPBOOK to organize that process.

## Wrapper

**Context** You are part of an active, long-running, and possibly quite complex project with more than a handful of participants. How do you manage? **The project presents a certain user interface to the world. If the primary interface is based on a simple leader/follower dichotomy, then it's easy to know where everyone stands. But peeragogy requires a more sophisticated facilitation/colearning dynamic.**

**Problem** In an active project, it can be effectively impossible to stay up to date with all of the details. Not everyone will be able to attend every meeting (see HEARTBEAT) or read every email. Project participants can easily get lost and drift away. The experience can be much more difficult for NEWCOMERS: joining an existing project can feel like trying to climb aboard a rapidly moving vehicle. If you've taken time off, you may feel like things have moved on so far that you cannot catch up. Information overload is not the only concern: there is also a problem with missing information. If they aren't shared, key skills can quickly become bottlenecks (see CARRYING CAPACITY).

**Solution** Someone involved with the project should regularly create a wrap-up summary, distinct from other project communications, that makes current activities comprehensible to people who may not have been following all of the details. In addition, project members should keep other informative resources like the landing page, ROADMAP, and documentation up to date. Ensure that these resources accurately represent the facts on the ground, and check empirically to see if they really show interested parties how they can get involved.

**Rationale** According to the theory proposed by Yochai Benkler, for free/open "commons-based" projects to work, it is important for participants to be able to contribute small pieces, and for the project to have a way to stitch those pieces together [1]. The WRAPPER helps perform this integrative stitching function. If you value participation, you may have to do some serious work to facilitate access to process.

**Resolution** Regularly circulated summaries can help to engage or re-engage members of a project, and can give an emotional boost to peeragogues who see their contributions and concerns mentioned. Well-maintained records chronicle the project's history; up-to-date documentation makes the project more robust; a coherent look-and-feel makes it accessible. In short, surfaces matter. People can tell the difference between a project that is led by example and one that is led by fiat; they can see right away if the project welcomes contributions with love, and if the participants feel they have something valuable to share.

**Example 1** There are many data streams around the Wikimedia project. They comprise an elaborate WRAPPER function for

Figure 6.4: Design for a Peeragogy project dashboard (design sketch by Amanda Lyons, prototype by Fabrizio Terzi).

the project, with components that range from Today's Featured Article, which appears on the front page of Wikipedia, to formal annual reports from the nonprofit. Wikipedia also plays a WRAPPER function in a broader sense. It is a typical first port of call for people searching for information about the world.

**Example 2** In-person meetings are no less relevant for contemporary humans than they were a century ago, even though we often work remotely, and have learned more about how to assemble on the fly [2]. Getting together for conventions, dance parties, and commencement ceremonies could comprise an important part of the future university's WRAPPER function, even if these events do not always take place in one specific Assembly Hall.

*What's Next.* We have prototyped and deployed a visual "dashboard" that people can use to get involved with the ongoing work in the project. Let's improve it, and match it with an improved interaction design for peeragogy.org.

### References

1. Y. Benkler. "Coase's Penguin, or Linux and the Nature of the Firm". In: *Yale Law Journal* 112 (2002), p. 369.
2. Howard Rheingold. *Smart mobs: The next social revolution.* Basic books, 2007.

## Heartbeat

**Context** A number of people have a shared interest, and have connected with each other about it. However, they are not going to spend 24 hours a day, 7 days a week working together, either because they are busy with other things, or because working separately on some tasks is vastly more efficient. **Even if we do spend lots of time together, it isn't all equally meaningful. Something needs to hold the project together, or it will fall apart.**

**Problem** How will the effort be sustained and coordinated sufficiently? How do we know this an active collaboration, and not just a bunch of people milling about? Is there a *there, there?*

**Solution** People seem to naturally gravitate to something with a pulse. *Once a day* (standups), *once a week* (meetings), or *once a year* (conferences, festivals) are common variants. When the project is populated by more than just a few people, it's likely that there will be several HEARTBEATS, building a sophisticated polyrhythm. A well-running project will feel "like an improvisational jazz ensemble" [1]. Much as the band director may gesture to specific players to invite them to solo or sync up, a project facilitator may craft individual emails to ask someone to lead an activity or invite them to re-engage. Two common rhythm components are weekly synchronous meetings with an open agenda, combined with *ad hoc* meetings for focused work on A SPECIFIC PROJECT. The precise details will depend on the degree of integration required by the group.

**Rationale** The project's heartbeat is what sustains it. Just as *people matter more than code* [2], so does the life of the working group matter more than mechanics of the work structure. Indeed, there is an quick way to do a reality check and find the project's strongest pulse: the activities that sustain a healthy project should sustain us, too (cf. CARRYING CAPACITY).

**Resolution** Used mindfully, the HEARTBEAT can be a sophisticated tool. Noticing when a new HEARTBEAT is beginning to emerge is a way to be aware of the shifting priorities in the group, and may be a good source of new patterns. Like a HEARTBEAT, patterns recur. On the other hand, if a specific activity is no longer sustaining the project, stop doing it, much as you would move an out-of-date pattern to the SCRAPBOOK in order to make room for other concerns. The power of the HEARTBEAT is that the project can be as focused and intensive as it needs to be.

**Example 1** The yearly in-person gathering, Wikimania, is the most visible example of a HEARTBEAT for the Wikimedia movement. Local chapters and projects may run additional in-person get-togethers. Also of note is the twice-yearly call for proposals for individual engagement grants.

**Example 2** Although it may sound quaint, working farms could help to physically sustain peeragogues, while putting the project's HEARTBEAT in tune with that of the seasons. In the current distributed mode, we tend our windowboxes and allotment gardens.

*What's Next.* Identifying and fostering new HEARTBEATS and new working groups is a task that can help make the community more robust. This is the time dimension of spin off projects described in REDUCE, REUSE, RECYCLE.

### References

1. David M. Dikel, David Kane, and James R. Wilson. *Software architecture: Organizational Principles and Patterns.* Pearson Education, 2001.
2. Linus Torvalds and Steven Vaughan-Nichols. *Linus Torvalds's Lessons on Software Development Management.* 2011. URL: http://web.archive.org/web/20131021211847/http://h30565.www3.hp.com/t5/Feature-Articles/Linus-Torvalds-s-Lessons-on-Software-Development-Management/ba-p/440.

## Newcomer

**Context** When there's learning happening, it's because there is someone who is new to a topic, or to something about the topic. **There is an 'invisible hand' in peeragogy that makes it so that each person pursuing his or her own optimal course of learning is what's best for the community. However, this does not isolate us from one another, but draws us together.**

**Problem** Newcomers can feel overwhelmed by the amount of things to learn. They don't know where to start. They may have a bunch of ideas that the oldtimers have never considered – or they may think they have new ideas, which are actually a different take on an old idea; see REDUCE, REUSE, RECYCLE. People who are new to the project can tell you what makes their participation difficult. Since you're learning as you go as well, you can ask yourself the same question: what aspects of this are difficult for me?

**Solution** In an active learning context, we render assistance to others more effectively when we do so as peers, rather than doing it as experts operating in a *provisionist* mode [1]. Instead of thinking of newcomers as "them", and trying to provide solutions, we focus on newcomers as "us" – which makes the search for solutions that much more urgent. We permit ourselves to ask naive questions. We entertain vague ideas. We add concreteness by trying A SPECIFIC PROJECT. We may then genuinely turn to others for help.

**Rationale** Sharing vulnerability and confusion gives us a chance to learn together. A newcomer's confusion about how best to get involved or what the point of all this actually is may be due to a lack of structure in the project ROADMAP, and it points to places where others in the project probably have something to learn too.

**Resolution** An awareness of the difficulties that newcomers face can help us be more compassionate to ourselves and others. We become open to new ideas, which can show how we have been limiting ourselves. Relative to the goals of effecting real change and enhancing the world's liveability, we really are beginners. We will have a better chance of making the project useful for others if we're clear about how it is useful to *us*.

**Example 1** Wikipedia NEWCOMERS can make use of resources that include a "Teahouse" where questions are welcomed, a platform extension that changes the user interface for new editors, and lots of documentation.[11] The efforts of exceptional newcomers may be given special recognition. Newcomer "survival" is of interest to the Wikimedia Foundation. The degree to which Wikimedia projects emphasize continuous upskilling (à la the NEWCOMER pattern) is somewhat less clear.

**Example 2** It will often be pragmatic to connect NEWCOMERS with employment, so that the future university may see a closer coupling of science and industry than is held in the former model. Inspiration can be drawn the London-based freelancing cooperative Founders&Coders, which is able to offer intensive training in web development at no cost to successful applicants, on the basis that some trainees will choose to join the cooperative as paying members later on.

*What's Next.* A more detailed (but non-limiting) "How to Get Involved" walk-through or "DIY Toolkit" would be good to develop. We can start by listing some of the things we're currently learning about.

### References

1. D. Boud and A. Lee. "'Peer learning' as pedagogic discourse for research education". In: *Studies in Higher Education* 30.5 (2005), pp. 501–516.

## Scrapbook

**Context** We've maintained and revised our pattern catalog over a period of years. We're achieving the "What's Next" steps attached to some of the patterns. **We have limited energy, and therefor need to ask: where should we set the focus?**

**Problem** Not all of the patterns we've noticed remain equally relevant. In particular, some of the patterns no longer lead to concrete next steps.

**Solution** In order to maintain focus, is important to "tune" and "prune" the collection of patterns receiving active attention. Connect this understanding to concrete actions undertaken in the project by frequently asking questions like these:

> (1) Review what was supposed to happen. (2) Establish what is happening/happened. (3) Determine what's right and wrong with what we are doing/have done. (4) What did we learn or change? (5) What else should we change going forward? [2, Chapter 28].

After reviewing our activities with respect to these questions, our current priorities will become clearer. If a particular pattern is no longer of current relevance, move it to a SCRAPBOOK. In addition to retired patterns, use the scrapbook to maintain a backlog, or "parking lot," of proto-patterns, in the form of outstanding problems, issues, and concerns. Don't limit yourself to *your own* creativity: include bookmarks to or clippings from patterns from other sources (see REDUCE, REUSE, RECYCLE).

**Rationale** We want our pattern catalog to be concretely useful and actively used, and to keep attention focused on the most relevant issues. If a pattern is not specifically useful or actionable at the moment, sufficient time for reflection may offer a better understanding, or it may prove useful in a different context.

**Resolution** Judicious use of the SCRAPBOOK can help focus project participants, and can make it easier to communicate current priorities to others in a clear manner. The currently active pattern catalog is leaner and more action-oriented as a result. A realistic and useful focus takes both the past and the future into account. If the ROADMAP shows where we're going, it is the SCRAPBOOK that shows most clearly where we've been.

**Example 1** Now that new plans are being formed, the Wikimedia Foundation's previous "five year plan" somewhat resembles a SCRAPBOOK [1].

**Example 2** In the future university, the patterns described here will continue to shape the landscape, but considerable activity will be focused on new problems and new patterns – just as a university campus grows and changes with the addition of new buildings.

*What's Next.* After pruning back our pattern catalog, we want it to grow again: new patterns are needed. One strategy would be to "patternize" the rest of the *Peeragogy Handbook.*

## References

1. Eugene Eric Kim et al. *Wikimedia Strategic Plan: A collaborative vision for the movement through 2015*. Wikimedia Foundation, 2011.
2. H. Rheingold et al. *The Peeragogy Handbook*. 3rd. Chicago, IL./Somerville, MA.: PubDomEd/Pierce Press, 2015. URL: http://peeragogy.org.

CHAPTER 7

# EMERGENT ROADMAP

This section reprises the "What's Next" steps from all of the previous patterns, offering another view on the Peeragogy project's ROADMAP in a concrete emergent form.

**Peeragogy** We intend to revise and extend the patterns and methods of peeragogy to make it a workable model for learning, inside or outside of institutions.

**Roadmap** If we sense that something needs to change about the project, that is a clue that we might need to record a new pattern, or revise our existing patterns.

**Reduce, reuse, recycle** We've converted our old pattern catalog from the *Peeragogy Handbook* into this paper, sharing it with a new community and gaining new perspectives. Can we repeat that for other things we've made?

**Carrying capacity** Making it easy and fruitful for others to get involved is one of the best ways to redistribute the load. This often requires skill development among those involved; compare the NEWCOMER pattern.

**A specific project** We need to build specific, tangible "what's next" steps and connect them with concrete action. Use the SCRAPBOOK to organize that process.

**Wrapper** We have prototyped and deployed a visual "dashboard" that people can use to get involved with the ongoing work in the project. Let's improve it, and match it with an improved interaction design for peeragogy.org.

**Heartbeat** Identifying and fostering new HEARTBEATS and new working groups is a task that can help make the community more robust. This is the time dimension of spin off projects described in REDUCE, REUSE, RECYCLE.

**Newcomer** A more detailed (but non-limiting) "How to Get Involved" walk-through or "DIY Toolkit" would be good to develop. We can start by listing some of the things we're currently learning about.

**Scrapbook** After pruning back our pattern catalog, we want it to grow again: new patterns are needed. One strategy would be to "patternize" the rest of the *Peeragogy Handbook*.

## Summary

We introduced nine patterns of peeragogy and connected them to concrete next steps for the Peeragogy project. In order to demonstrate the generality of these patterns, we included examples showing how they manifest in current Wikimedia projects, and how the patterns could inform the design of a future university rooted in the values and methods of peer production. We will close by reviewing our contribution using three dimensions of analysis borrowed from [1].

**Organization** Managing work on our project with design patterns that are augmented with a "What's next" follow through step *decentralizes both goal setting and execution* [1], reintegrating structure in the form of an emergent ROADMAP. We have aimed to make our discussion general and our methods extensible enough to work at varied levels of scale and degrees of formality, inside or outside of institutional frameworks.

**Motivation** The future university may be the Chartes of programming, but it will have plenty in common with the bazaar [3]. As P2PU cofounder Philipp Schmidt indicates, *learning is at the* *core of peer production communities* [4]. Our patterns help to explicate the way these communities work, but more importantly, we hope they will foment a culture of learning.

**Quality** "By intervening in real communities, these efforts achieve a level of external validity that lab-based experiments cannot" [1]. The "What's next" annotation piloted here will be helpful to other design pattern authors who aim to use patterns as part of a research intervention. Peer production is not guaranteed to out-compete proprietary solutions [1, 2]; its potential for success will depend on the way problems are framed, and our ability to follow through.

## References


1. Yochai Benkler, Aaron Shaw, and Benjamin Mako Hill. "Peer production: a modality of collective intelligence". In: *The Collective Intelligence Handbook*. Ed. by Thomas W. Malone and Michael S. Bernstein. To appear. MIT Press, 2015.
2. Benjamin Mako Hill. *When Free Software Isn't (Practically) Better.* Published on gnu.org. Licensed via CC-By-SA. 2011. URL: `http://www.gnu.org/philosophy/when_free_software_isnt_practically_better.html`.
3. Eric S Raymond. *The Cathedral & the Bazaar: Musings on Linux and open source by an accidental revolutionary.* O'Reilly Media, Inc., 2001.
4. J. P. Schmidt. "Commons-Based Peer Production and education". In: *Free Culture Research Workshop, Harvard University* (2009), 3 pp. URL: `http://cyber.law.harvard.edu/fcrw/sites/fcrw/images/Schmidt_Education_FreeCulture_25Oct2009.pdf`.

CHAPTER 8

# CASE STUDY: SWATS

Miguel Ángel Pérez Álvarez & Elisa Armendáriz
*with*
Paola Ricuarte & Joseph Corneli

Learning to use technology with peers – the case of Students With Abilities in Technology (SWATs).

## Part 1: Introduction

Mind-amplifying technologies [1], technologies of cooperation [2], such as conversation technologies, as well as visualization tools, video and photo edition software, simulators or programming technologies are emerging learning tools in schools around the world. They are affordable and accessible enough to design learning environments. Latin America is no exception and it is fast becoming the norm to find convergent technology in the classroom.

We challenged students to develop a three-level game with a score or marker using Scratch, a program developed by the MIT. This program allows you to develop computer programs using modules or blocks of instructions. The educational value of this tool lies not in its ease of use but in its nature as an authentic learning environment and ideal context for developing intellectual skills.

Once students have developed their programs and documented the process in a learning log, we asked them if they had faced problems in handling Scratch. In this way we were able to identify which students had difficulties in developing programs and what their problems were in the process of choosing instructions. However, we're also able to identify those students with particular technical skills. We call them Students With Abilities in Technology (SWATs). In case of difficulty, SWATs can be called in, and can decide if they want to give advice to peers and the teacher in the use of Scratch.

The idea of identifying these students and asking them to support their peers and teachers in specific tasks has an additional educational component. It is clear that when a student is given the task of explaining or advising peers or teachers, he develops new competences and masters, to an even greater extent, those competences for which he/she was selected as SWAT.

We have observationally determined that this approach is relevant to the widespread use of digital devices in academic tasks and its extended application contributes to a more positive use of digital technologies for learning. We see how, as the use of technology in all learning environments becomes general, this approach of peer learning becomes an alternative to underpin the work of teachers. The figure of the SWAT in the classroom also enables a different form of relationship between pairs that generate new forms of interaction and learning that we can appraise and evaluate.

## Part 2. Representation as a pattern

Here's how the short case study could be described using the pattern template that we've presented in the book. It's pretty easy to turn a case study into a design pattern!

**Title:** Students With Abilities in Technology (SWATs)

**Context:** Private and public schools increasingly have digital devices in classrooms with Internet access (laptops, desktops, tablets, cell phones, etc.) and **teachers with little or no expertise in the educational use of such devices** . Furthermore, the teachers are often embedded in a **framework for teaching and learning** that doesn't take into account the "horizontal" modes of thinking that modern technology enables. **However, some of**

**the students do have considerable background with these kinds of tools.**

**Problem:** In general, teachers have multiple deficiencies in the adoption of emerging technologies. Their lack of expertise prevents them from realizing the full potential that technology has as a relevant pedagogical mediation. The rate of change in the school context, however, is not coupled to the rate of change in current teacher training programs. This lack of pedagogical training is having a majorly disruptive impact in the classroom given this presence of technological devices in the classroom. The reaction of administrators and teachers to the proliferation of devices is, in a significant number of cases, rejection and stigmatization of emerging technologies. Teachers may be ignoring the educational potential of technology, and ignoring the way technology has changed the cognitive model of a whole generation. Having paid technical specialists to support the work of the teacher in the classroom is unthinkable from an economic standpoint.

**Solution:** The students themselves can be the solution to this problem. Some have superior technical knowledge and this is usually wasted. Teachers can incorporate them as assistants to help them and their peers. A student with digital skills can be the agent of change that many teachers need in order to learn how to use technology for the design of learning environments. This empowered group of students, that we named SWAT (Students With Abilities in Technology) support teachers and peers with lower-level digital competences. Support from students with technical knowledge could mean a significant change in the learning process, because teachers can now combine that knowledge with their teaching experience and pedagogical strategies. The result of this can be the discovery of the many possibilities technology has for the construction of knowledge and the development of new intellectual abilities.

In our work with middle school students (ages 12-14), the support of SWATs inside and outside the classroom was a very positive experience. At the beginning of each course students are required to develop projects involving the use of technology. Students who show a greater competence in the use of technical tools are invited to join as SWAT. Once SWATs are identified, they are asked regarding the possibility of supporting teachers and their peers in the use of specific computer tools. It is impressive to see teachers becoming co-learners who take advantage of this privileged status of their students to master tools that promote their ability to redesign learning environments. When students need support for developing their projects, SWATs show them strategies to accomplish them. The majority report great pleasure and pride in their new role as peer advisors.

**Rationale:** This peeragogical approach changes the prevailing educational paradigm through collaboration between teachers and students, and among students themselves. There are many possible points of friction (which is not necessarily a bad thing). To have one or more SWATs in each learning group transforms the way in which teachers and students interact with each other and with available technologies. This can create challenges for teachers who may be used to a more "banking" style of teaching (again, not a bad thing in and of itself). In order for teachers who are new to peer learning to become more comfortable with a shifting balance of power, they will need to have access to the overall ROADMAP.

**Resolution:** SWATs can help the teachers and other students with technical issues. This goes along with another social result: injecting some peer learning into an otherwise hierarchical setting.

*What's Next.* Can we help ways to engage with SWATs to help them become even more proficient with technology, offering them some mentoring in exchange for help with our project?

## References

1. Howard Rheingold (2012), "Mind Amplifier: Can Our Digital Tools Make Us Smarter?"
2. Instute of the Future (2005), "Technology of cooperation"

# Part IV

# Convening A Group

CHAPTER 9

# SO YOU'VE DECIDED TO TRY PEER LEARNING...

GIGI JOHNSON

So you've decided you to try peer learning? Great! Maybe you've already found a few people who will support you in this effort. Congratulations! It's time now to focus your thinking. How will you convene others to form a suitable group? How will you design a learner experience which will make your project thrive? In this chapter, we suggest a variety of questions that will help you to make your project more concrete for potential new members. There are no good or bad answers - it depends on the nature of your project and the context. Trying to answer the questions is not something you do just once. At various stages of the project, even after it's over, some or all of those questions will aquire new meanings - and probably new answers.

> **Fabrizio Terzi**: "There is a force of attraction that allows aggregation into groups based on the degree of personal interest; the ability to enhance and improve the share of each participant; the expectation of success and potential benefit."

## Group identity

Note that there are many groups that may not need to be "convened", since they already exist. There is a good story from A. T. Ariyaratne in his collected works in which he does "convene" a natural group (a village) - but in any case, keep in mind at the outset that the degree of group-consciousness that is necessary for peer learning to take place is not fixed. In this section, we suppose you are just at the point of kicking off a project. What steps should you take? We suggest you take a moment to ponder the following questions first - and revisit them afterward, as a way to identify best practices for the next effort.

## There will be a quiz

Those taking the initiative should ask themselves the traditional Who, What, Where, When, Why, and How. (Simon Sinek suggests to begin with Why, and we touched on Who, above!). In doing so, preliminary assumptions for design and structure are established. However, in peer learning it is particularly important to maintain a healthy degree of openness, so that future group members can also form their answers on those questions. In particular, this suggests that the design and structure of the project (and the group) may change over time. Here, we riff on the traditional 5W's+H with six clusters of questions to help you focus your thinking about the project and amplify its positive outcomes.

## Expectations for participants

### 1. Who: Roles and flux

- What are some of the roles that people are likely to fall into (e.g. Newcomer, Wrapper, Lurker, Aggregator, etc.)?
- How likely is it that participants will stick with the project? If you expect many participants to leave, how will this effect the group and the outcome?
- Do you envision new people joining the group as time goes by? If so, what features are you designing that will support their integration into an existing flow?
- Will the project work if people dip in and out? If so, what features support that? If not, how will people stay focused?

### 2. What: Nature of the project

- What skills are required? What skills are you trying to build?
- What kinds of change will participants undergo? Will they be heading into new ground? Changing their minds about something? Learning about learning?
- What social objective, or "product" if any, is the project aiming to achieve?
- What's the 'hook?' Unless you are working with an existing group, or re-using an existing modality, consistent participation may not be a given.

### 3. When: Time management

- What do you expect the group to do, from the moment it convenes, to the end of its life-span, to create the specific outcome that will exist at the conclusion of its last meeting? [2] Note that what people ACTUALLY do may be different from what you envision at the outset, so you may want to revisit this question (and your answer) again as the project progresses.
- Keeping in mind that at least one period of is inertia is very likely [2], what event(s) do you anticipate happening in the group that will bring things back together, set a new direction, or generally get things on track? More generally, what kinds of contingencies does your group face? How does it interface to the "outside world"?
- What pre-existing narratives or workflows could you copy in your group?
- How much of a time commitment do you expect from participants? Is this kind of commitment realistic for members of your group?
- What, if anything, can you do to make participation "easy" in the sense that it happens in the natural flow of life for group members?

- Does everyone need to participate equally? How might non-equal participation play out for participants down the line?

### 4. Where: Journey vs Destination

- What structures will support participants in their journey to the end result(s) you (or they) have envisioned? What content can you use to flesh out this structure?
- Where can the structure "flex" to accommodate unknown developments or needs as participants learn, discover, and progress?

### 5. Why: Tool/platform choice

- What tools are particularly suited to this group? Consider such features as learning styles and experiences, geographical diversity, the need for centralization (or decentralization), cultural expectations related to group work, sharing, and emerging leadership.
- Is there an inherent draw to this project for a given population, or are you as facilitator going to have to work at keeping people involved? How might your answer influence your choice of tools? Is the reward for completion the learning itself, or something more tangible?
- In choosing tools, how do you prioritize such values and objectives as easy entry, diverse uses, and high ceilings for sophisticated expansion?

### 6. How: Linearity vs Messiness

- How will your group manage feedback in a constructive way?
- Why might participants feel motivated to give feedback?
- How firm and extensive are the social contracts for this group? Do they apply to everyone equally, or do they vary with participation level?

- What do people need to know at the start? What can you work out as you go along? Who decides?
- How welcome are "meta-discussions"? What kinds of discussions are not likely to be welcome? Do you have facilities in place for "breakout groups" or other peer-to-peer interactions? (Alternatively, if the project is mostly distributed, do you have any facilities in place for coming together as a group?)

## Cycles of group development

The above questions remain important thoughout the life of the project. People may come and go, particpants may propose fundamentally new approaches, people may evolve from lurkers to major content creators or vice-versa. The questions we suggest can be most effective if your group discusses them over time, as part of its workflow, using synchronous online meetings (e.g., Big Blue Button, Adobe Connect, Blackboard Collaborate), forums, Google docs, wikis, and/or email lists. Regular meetings are one way to establish a "heartbeat" for the group.

In thinking about other ways of structuring things, note that the "body" of the *Peeragogy Handbook* follows a Tuckman-like outline (*Convening a Group* is our "forming", *Organizing a Learning Context* is our "storming and norming", *Co-working/Facilitation* is our "performing", and *Assessment* is our "adjourning"). But we agree with Gersick [1], and Engeström [2], that groups do not always follow a linear or cyclical pattern with their activities!

Nevertheless, there may be some specific stages or phases that you want *your* group to go through. Do you need some "milestones," for example? How will you know when you've achieved "success?"

In closing, it is worth reminding you that it is natural for groups to experience conflict, especially as they grow or cross other threshold points or milestones - or perhaps more likely, when they don't cross important milestones in a timely fashion (ah, so you remember those milestones from the previous section!). Nevertheless, there are some strategies can be used to make this conflict productive, rather than merely destructive (see Ozturk and Simsek [3]).

## References

1. Gersick, C. (1988). Time and transition in work teams: Toward a new model of group development. *Academy of Management Journal* 31 (Oct.): 9-41.
2. Engeström, Y. (1999). Innovative learning in work teams: Analyzing cycles of knowledge creation in practice. In Y. Engeström, R. Miettinen & R.-L-. Punamäki (Eds.), *Perspectives on activity theory*, (pp. 377-404). Cambridge, UK: Cambridge University Press.
3. Ozturk and Simsek (2012). "Of Conflict in Virtual Learning Communities in the Context of a Democratic Pedagogy: A paradox or sophism?," in *Proceedings of the Networked Learning Conference, 2012, Maastricht.* (Video or text.)

CHAPTER 10

# PLAY AND LEARNING

Bryan Alexander & Anna Keune

Once more we're back to the question, "What makes learning fun?" There are deep links between play and learning. Consider, for instance, the way we learn the rules of a game through playing it. The first times we play a card game, or a physical sport, or a computer simulation we test out rule boundaries as well as our understanding. Actors and role-players learn their roles through the dynamic process of performance. The resulting learning isn't absorbed all at once, but accretes over time through an emergent process, one unfolding further through iterations. In other words, the more we play a game, the more we learn it.

In addition to the rules of play, we learn about the subject which play represents, be it a strategy game (chess, for example) or simulation of economic conflict. Good games echo good teaching practice, too, in that they structure a single player's experience to fit their regime of competence (cf. Vygotsky's zone of proximal learning, a la Gee [1]). That is to say a game challenges players at a level suited to their skill and knowledge: comfortable enough that play is possible, but so challenging as to avoid boredom, eliciting player growth. Role-playing in theater lets performers explore and test out concepts; see Boal [2]. Further, adopting a playful attitude helps individuals meet new challenges with curiousity, along with a readiness to mobilize ideas and practical knowledge. Indeed, the energy activated by play can take a person beyond an event's formal limitations, as players can assume that play can go on and on [3].

**Douglas Thomas and John Seely Brown**: "All systems of play are, at base, learning systems." [4]

Games have always had a major social component, and learning plays a key role in that interpersonal function. Using games to build group cohesion is an old practice, actually a triusm in team sports.

It is important to locate our peeragogical moment in a world where gaming is undergoing a renaissance. Not only has digital gaming become a large industry, but gaming has begun to infiltrate non-gaming aspects of the world, sometimes referred to as "gamification." Putting all three of these levels together, we see that we can possibly improve co-learning by adopting a playful mindset. Such a playful attitude can then mobilize any or all of the above advantages. For example,

- Two friends are learning the Russian language together. They invent a vocabulary game: one identifies an object in the world, and the other must name it in Russian. They take turns, each challenging the other, building up their common knowledge.
- A middle-aged man decides to take up hiking. The prospect is somewhat daunting, since he's a very proud person and is easily stymied by learning something from scratch. So he adopts a "trail name", a playful pseudonym. This new identity lets him set-aside his self-importance and risk making mistakes. Gradually he grows comfortable with what his new persona learns.
- We can also consider the **design** field as a useful kind of playful peeragogy. The person *playing the role* of the designer can select the contextual frame within which the design is performed. This frame can be seen as the *rules* governing the design, the artifact and the process. These rules, as with some games, may change over time. Therefore the possibility to adapt, to tailor one's activities to changing context is important when designing playful learning activities. (And we'll look at some ways to design peer learning experiences next!)

Of course, "game-based learning" can be part of standard pedagogy too. When peers create the game themselves, this presumably involves both game-based learning and peer learning. Classic strategy games like Go and Chess also provide clear examples of peer learning practices: the question is partly, what skills and mindsets do our game-related practices really teach?

> **Socrates**: "No compulsory learning can remain in the soul ... In teaching children, train them by a kind of game, and you will be able to see more clearly the natural bent of each."
>
> Quoted by Thomas Malone [5].

### Exercises that can help you cultivate a playful attitude

- Use the Oblique Strategies card deck (Brian Eno and Peter Schmidt, 1st edition 1975, now available in its fifth edition) to spur playful creativity. Each card advises players to change their creative process, often in surprising directions.
- Take turns making and sharing videos. This online collaborative continuous video storytelling involves a group of people creating short videos, uploading them to YouTube, then making playlists of results. Similar to Clip Kino, only online.
- Engage in theater play using Google+ Hangout. e.g. coming together with a group of people online and performing theatrical performances on a shared topic that are recorded.

## References

1. Gee, J. P. (1992). *The social mind: Language, ideology, and social practice.* Series in language and ideology. New York: Bergin & Garvey.
2. Boal, A. (1979). *Theatre of the oppressed.* 3rd ed. London: Pluto Press.
3. Bereiter, C. and Scadamalia, M. (1993). *Surpassing ourselves, an inquiry into the nature and implications of expertise.* Peru, Illinois: Open Court.

4. Douglas Thomas and John Seely Brown (2011), *A New Culture of Learning: Cultivating the Imagination for a World of Constant Change.* CreateSpace.
5. Malone, T.W. (1981), Toward a Theory of Intrinsically Motivating Instruction, *Cognitive Science*, 4, pp. 333-369

CHAPTER 11

# K-12 PEERAGOGY

VERENA ROBERTS

Teachers have a reputation of working in isolation, of keeping their learning to themselves and on their own islands. They are also known for generously sharing resources with one another. It is this latter trait that is becoming increasingly important as the role of the educator continues to expand. As educational technology research specialist Stephen Downes observes, the expectations on teachers have grown from "being expert in the discipline of teaching and pedagogy...[to needing to have] up-to-date and relevant knowledge and experience in it. Even a teacher of basic disciplines such as science, history or mathematics must remain grounded, as no discipline has remained stable for very long, and all disciplines require a deeper insight in order to be taught effectively." It is no longer possible for an educator to work alone to fulfil each of these roles: the solution is to work and learn in collaboration with others. This is where peer-based sharing and learning online, connected/networked learning, or peeragogy, can play an important role in helping educators.

## Becoming a connected/networked learner

The following steps are set out in 'phases' in order to suggest possible experiences one may encounter when becoming connected. It is acknowledged that every learner is different and these 'phases' only serve as a guide.

### Phase 1: Deciding to take the plunge

To help educators begin to connect, the Connected Educator's Starter Kit was created during Connected Educator's Month in

August 2012. This article previews the main steps. The first step to becoming a 'connected educator-learner' involves making the commitment to spending the time you'll need to learn how to learn and share in an open, connected environment.

### Phase 2: Lurking

We start off as lurkers. A learner can be considered a true 'lurker' after reviewing the starter kit, establishing a digital presence (through a blog or a wiki) or signing up for Twitter and creating a basic profile containing a photo. In this phase, lurkers will begin to 'follow' other users on Twitter and observe educational Twitter 'chats'. Lurkers will also begin to seek out other resources through blogs, Facebook, Edmodo and LinkedIn groups.

### Phase 3: Entering the fray

The lurker begins to develop into a connected educator-learner once he or she makes the decision to enter into a dialogue with another user. This could take the form of a personal blog post, participation on an education-related blog or wiki or a an exchange with another Twitter user. Once this exchange takes place, relationships may begin to form and the work towards building a Personal Learning Network (PLN) begins.

One such site where such relationships can be built is Classroom 2.0, which was founded by Steve Hargadon. Through Classroom 2.0, Steve facilitates a number of free online learning opportunities including weekly Blackboard Collaborate sessions, conferences, book projects and grassroots cross-country educational-transformation tours. Classroom 2.0 also offers a supportive Social Ning—a free, social learning space that provides online conferences and synchronous and recorded interviews with inspirational educators—for connected educator-learners around the world.

### Phase 4: Building and shaping your PLN

Just as not every person one meets becomes a friend, it is important to remember that not every exchange will lead to a co-learning peeragogy arrangement. It may be sufficient to follow another who provides useful content without expecting any reciprocation. It is dependent on each educator-learner to determine who to pay attention to and what learning purpose that individual or group will serve. It is also up to the learner-educator to demonstrate to others that he or she will actively participate.

There are a number of strategies one can use when shaping the PLN to learn. However, one of the best ways educators can attract a core of *peeragogues* is by sharing actively and demonstrating active and open learning for others.

There are a number of sites where a new educator-learner can actively and openly learn. In addition to personal blogging and wikis, other professional development opportunities include open, online courses and weekly synchronous online meetings through video, podcasts or other forms of media.

Examples include: Connected Learning TV, TechTalkTuesdays, VolunteersNeeded, SimpleK12, K12 Online, CEET, and EdTechTalk.

Alternatively, courses are offered with P2PU's School of Education or a wide variety of other opportunities collected by TeachThought and Educator's CPD online. Peggy George, the co-faciliator of the weekly Classroom 2.0 LIVE Sessions, created a livebinder package of free 'PD On Demand' connected professional development online options for peeragogy enthusiasts.

### Stage 5: Extending the digital PLN and connecting face-to-face

Over time, once the connected educator-learner has established a refined PLN, these peeragogues may choose to shift their learning into physical learning spaces. Some options available for these educator-learners would include the new 'grassroots unconferences', which include examples such as: EduCon, EdCamps, THATcamp and ConnectedCA.

These (un)conferences are free or extremely low-cost and focus on learning from and with others. These 'unconferences' are typically publicized through Twitter, Google Apps, and Facebook. Connecting face-to-face with other peeragogues can strengthen bonds to learning networks and help to promote their sustainability.

## Postscript

Sylvia Tolisano, Rodd Lucier and Zoe Branigan-Pipen co-created an infographic that which explores the experiences individuals may encounter in the journey to become connected learners through another related sequence of steps: *Lurker*, *Novice*, *Insider*, *Colleague*, *Collaborator*, *Friend*, and *Confidant*. Googlize it, and have a look at our Recommended Readings for some additional resources.

CHAPTER 12

# P2P SELF-ORGANIZED LEARNING ENVIRONMENTS

Jan Herder

From this conversational piece you can engage in a journey to affect your learning space through many points of entry interacting with the physical one. We hope to inspire emerging structure and reciprocal mentoring to create a ripple effect for those willing to open the door to a new possible world.

## The Guiding Strategy:

In his Peeragogical Case Study David Preston states:

> *Peeragogical interaction requires refining relational and topical critique, as well as skills in other "meta" literacies, including but not limited to critical thinking, collaboration, conflict resolution, decision-making, mindfulness, patience and compassion.*
>
> From "Case Study: 5PH1NX" (this volume).

A Self-Organizing Learning Environment, or SOLE, with a living structure accomplishes all of these outcomes, or David's "meta-literacies," simultaneously. An authentic problem and/or project based activity in a connected learning environment includes diverse learners in diverse ways by empowering all learners as peers.

This provides the authentic learning environment with which to design a SOLE. SOLEs are everywhere. How have we evolved as a species, if not through self-organizing? A conversation between strangers is self organizing, each learning about something

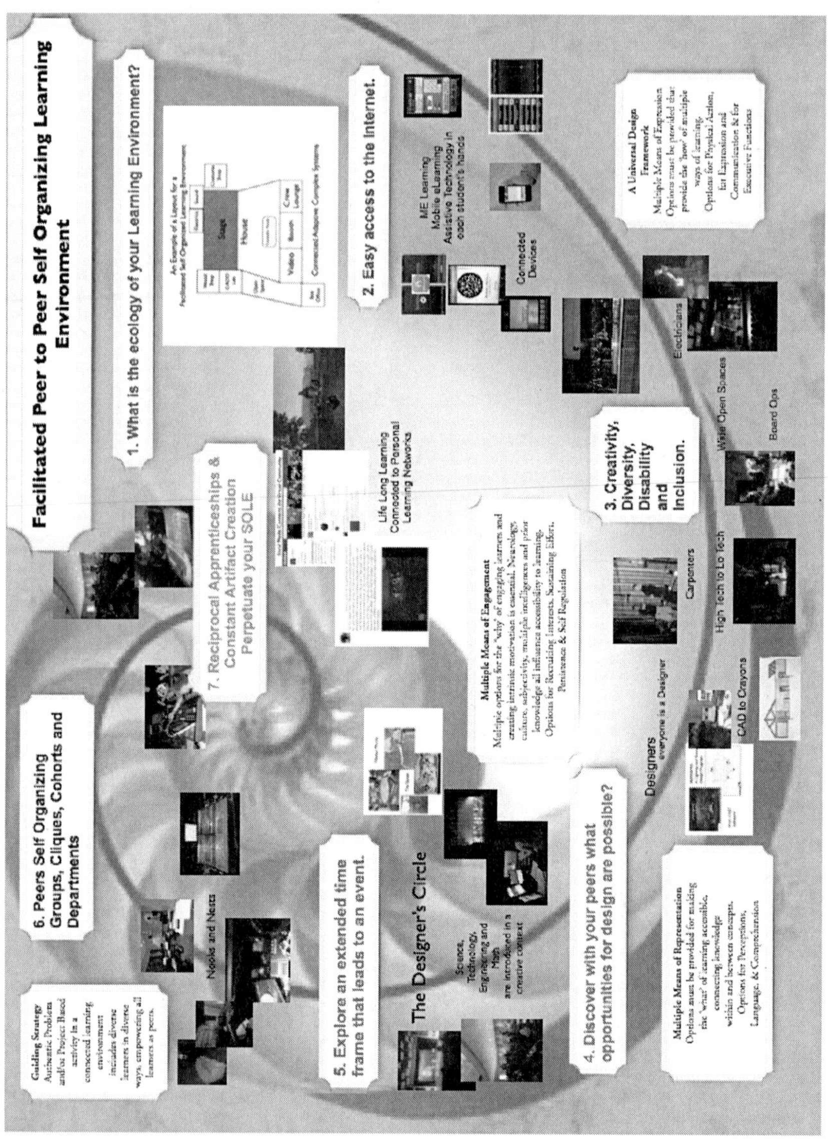


A visualization of the facilitated peer to peer SOLE, full-size at `http://goo.gl/7StkJK`

or each other. The spaces around people conversing is also an environment, though not explicitly a learning one. While we are always self-organizing to learn or accomplish things, one place that SOLEs do not always exist are in learning institutions. In many educational institutions, our learning environments are predominately organized by the teacher, curriculum, or society. How can we nurture peer to peer learning environments to organize? How does the role of the teacher differ in a SOLE? In what ways can we unite that fundamental, passionate human characteristic of curiosity and self-organizing back into our Learning Environments?

The model that Sugata Mitra [2] is experimenting with gives us some scaffolding to create one ourselves. This is the goal of his SOLE Tool Kit (3). Sugata's kit is directed towards children between 8 and 12 years old. I was wondering if there is a way to make it more universal in its application. How can I apply it to my situation? How is a SOLE different in the context of peer to peer learning? This chapter of the Handbook uses Sugata's model as a doorway into our understanding a SOLE approach to peer to peer learning. Its three key components are: learners, context and project. I find the discussion needs to integrate what we are learning about diverse learners into a Universal Design for Learning [4] context. After all, we cannot take for granted who the peers are in the SOLE. Equally, the context, the learning environment (LE) must be as deeply considered as the learners participating. As a learning designer, I am also seeking more clues about the living structure of a well crafted SOLE.

## Centers within the Center

SOLEs exist in a particular context. Take Sugata's hole in the wall [5] experiment. The parameters of the environment of a computer embedded in a wall in India are very specific. Sugata's act was to design a project in order to facilitate a process within that environment. The elements he introduced were a touch screen computer embedded in a wall with specific software. Sugata has abstracted this design into a Tool Kit. He speaks of 'Child Driven

Learning', intrinsically motivated learning with the curiosity to learn something in particular. As a learner-centric peeragogy, SOLEs are emergent, bottom up, seeking to answer: How do we design a project (or phrase a problem) that ignites a learner's passion?

A SOLE is a facilitated learning environment (LE) that can nurture learner driven activity. For instance, in the Hole in the Wall example, the design is the context of the wall, the street, the neighborhood –and the facilitation is the touch screen monitor in the wall. They are brilliantly united. In this sense it is an intentional, self-aware learning environment. It is a strange foreign object that anyone would have to figure out how it works to take advantage of. But this is not in the classroom, or in the 'school.' It is an informal LE. Just like learning a game [6], there is an entire ecology that surrounds you. This is very much a systemic approach. The context is facilitated explicitly (your design of the SOLE), but also implicitly in the hidden curriculum [7] that defines your LE. Above is the layout of the transformed learning environment [8] I explored to work around the hidden curriculum of the traditional classroom. The LE has a tremendous, if not overwhelming influence, on learning [9]. The first step in connected learning is to reconnect to the environment around us. For me, the primary context of my LE is a performing arts center at a small rural liberal arts college. The Performing Arts Center is a Center within the context of the college and community. A diversity of spaces within the facility are inhabited: small and cozy, large and public, technology embedded everywhere, all focused on the project based learning that emerges producing a performance. I stay away from a formal classroom as much as possible. These spaces are Centers within the Center, 'loosely connected adaptive complex systems' [10] within themselves, just like people. I believe that the possibility of a SOLE emerging as a living structure seems to depend on the correct types of complex systems engaged in the LE.

What is the role of the internet in your design? Mitigating inequalities and accommodating diverse learners are somewhat assisted by access to the internet. But it is the immediate, just-in-time learning [11] that makes free and open access to the world wide web so important in a SOLE. Wireless is available throughout this LE. Nooks and lounges, interconnected, but separate rooms, provide lots of places for collaboration or solitary work, for staying connected or hiding out. In a UDL vision of a facilitated peer to peer SOLE, technology is integral to the design. In the case of my LE, with the use of digital audio, multi-media, database management, robotic lighting and dichroic [12] colors, learners are accustomed to accessing and augmenting reality with technology: allowing learners to access their social media is part of their content creation.

Do we start our SOLE as peers? Peer to peer assumes your participants are peers–especially you, the facilitator. There needs to be enough diversity and complexity to include all learners, engendering a Universally Designed Context [13]. What is the role of diversity in peer to peer SOLE building? How are diverse learners peers? In my LE, I discovered 70% of my learners have learning challenges. I know my LE is not unique in this regard. I have to facilitate a SOLE design that is inclusive. This is in contradistinction to commonality, yet this diversity is what we crave, for creativity and innovation, for deep learning to occur. Crafting your SOLE using multiple means of representation, expression and engagement empowers learners to be peers. A diverse learning environment, supporting diverse learning styles and diverse learners, supports a complex project based SOLE. But there are many SOLEs within the SOLE since learning is occurring on many levels with each student and within each group. We do not all get the same thing at the same time. Learning outcomes are diverse, emergent, serendipitous.

What type of project, problem or event will focus your efforts? Either a learner generated syllabus [14] may emerge from the SOLE, or a user generated education [15] within a specific context may answer this question. Ownership and leadership emerge when learners can apply their creativity and/or authentically assist each other in a common goal. Opportunities to design and modify even small things will draw learners into a project. The more they must rely on each other, collaborate and share their creativity, their designs and actualization–the more they work together as peers. The spaces in your LE are most likely already designed and built to accommodate the purpose of the facility in the context of the college or school. We cannot really redesign the actual space, but we can redesign many aspects. We can look for designs within it. Being able to design your own space, or project, is critical to taking ownership of your learning and experiencing the consequences. As learners mature and look for ways to be more involved, I suggest they redesign the shop, the repertory lighting plot, or the procedures of their department and/or SOLE overall. Exchanging roles as designer also stimulates peer interaction. Why not integrate design and design thinking? In my context, lighting, scene, costume and sound design are interconnected opportunities. Along with accompanying technology, every opportunity is used to nurture empathy, creativity, rationality and systems thinking. Integral to the learner generated syllabus or project design should be continuous artifact creation. A great place to start the design process and to begin to generate content is by using a virtual world.

Constant content creation can integrate assessment into your SOLE. It is the quality of the artifacts created along the way that reveals the success of your SOLE. Media that chronicles a journey through time, created by each learner, reveals the depth of participation. It is nearly impossible to cheat. The learner expresses their comprehension in the types and extent of artifact creation.

As the facilitator, I look for opportunities to introduce the unexpected, bigger questions, deeper considerations, along the way. For example, in the context of my LE, one of the events feature Tibetan Monks. They bring a counterpoint to the inflated egos and cult of personality which is prevalent in our context. The SOLE Plan is extended. It can happen over a much longer amount of time than one class or one day. The actors rehearse for weeks, as the design team designs, giving time for: research, absorption, misleads, mistakes, correction and reflection. A SOLE needs time and persistence to generate artifacts, documentation and experiences of the project and virtual worlds are an excellent way to extend time and space synchronously and asynchronously.

Sugata emphasizes the Big questions. We do not always know what they are. A focus? A goal? A product? And the event? That should be decided with the group. The learners intuit the direction that leads to deep engagement and the bigger questions. I try and leave it ambiguous, suggesting some of the things they might encounter. Facilitating the SOLE in this context, we face endless questions connected to the specific LE, to all the imaginary scenarios, Herculean tasks and questions– like building castles, programming a digital sound console, troubleshooting robotic lighting instruments, how to make the illusion of fire or, even, who killed Charlemagne? The Box Office is an example of an informal SOLE that has emerged recurrently over time. I have noticed that its vitality depends on the characters and the ebb and flow of learners entering the group or graduating. The physical space is a small, windowless and often damp room with a couple of couches and a desk with a computer squeezed in. My very own 'Hole in the Wall' experiment. The bottom of the door can remain closed, while the top is open, like a stable. Primarily the students are paid to be there, answering the phone, reserving tickets, greeting patrons and managing the Box Office and the Front of the House. In the SOLE, this subtle inversion of the institutional value proposition turns 'work study' into studying work. This is an informal LE nested within the context of the formal institution and the wider LE: a center within a center. Some semesters there are business majors working their way up the job ladder: Usher to Assistant Front of House Manager, to Assistant Box Office Manager, to Box Office Manager. Sometimes this takes 4 years, sometimes it happens in a semester or two. It is a recursive SOLE that differs as the interests and skills of the students who inhabit the space change. As the current manager puts it, the Box Office is a 'constantly evolving puzzle.'

This example of a SOLE in an informal LE is similar to the other types of SOLE's that occur within a facilitated LE. The learner's interact as reciprocal apprentices, leaning on one another to solve challenges and problems. Groups are self-selective, this type of work suits their temperament and interests, or time. This cohort is almost a clique, attracting their boyfriends and girlfriends. They begin initiatives, re-design the lobby for crowd control, redecorate and rearrange the space constantly, decide their schedules and split up responsibility. Everyone is always training everyone, because the environment turns over each semester. It is explicitly an informal LE. The workers are students. This inverts the usual state of affairs, where essentially they are being paid to learn, though they may not even be aware of it. Occasionally, the learning experience resonates deeply with them. A number of them have used the experience to leverage jobs that parallel their interests, or get them started on their careers.

Job titles, roles of responsibility, are often problematic in a SOLE. The bottom line is that as peers we are all equal and at certain times everyone is expected to do everything regardless of their roles. Titles go to people's heads. But this is part of the experience. Keep the titles moving, change it up when things get bottlenecked over personalities. Sometimes I create duplicate positions, Assistants of Assistants. and Department Heads. The Apprenticeship model is at play but in a new way in a SOLE. There are peers and there are peers. As power struggles emerge, some like-to-like grouping occurs. The role of the facilitator becomes mediator. The emergent epistemology of abundance and connected learning asks for a multitude of 'experts.' In the same way, leadership can be distributed, flowing as varying needs arise.

The experience of practicing leadership skills and encountering all the variables of working with diverse folks quickly gives feedback to us if this is a helpful role for this person. It is messy sometimes, and there are conflicts. After a few events, they learn how to manage a Box Office, dealing with patrons, emergencies, complaints and bag check. They confront the larger peer group, the student body, with authority and empathy. They are very proud of their jobs and make their own name tags with titles. A hierarchy gives them rewards that they have been trained to expect from years in school. It is another way of developing intrinsic motivation and challenges them to interact with their peers authentically.

As facilitator, I try to leave them alone as much as possible. The context has been created, the computer in the wall is on a desk. Extending the design of your SOLE contributes to its living structure. I have used Facebook as a Supplemental LMS [16] since 2007 because this is where my students are and it allows them to control the structures of groups emergently. The learners create the groups as they are relevant. The facilitator does not. Usually they invite me in! For now, Facebook aggregates the learning community that the SOLE inspires as learners become leaders, establish connections with each other and mentor newbies. This activity is integrated into artifact creation, 'comments' and documentation of their personal learning journey. Facebook becomes a precursor for their portfolios, and in some cases, it is their portfolio. Reciprocal Apprenticeships [17] occur in the dynamic of collaboration among peers. Continuity in time beyond the event horizon is accomplished by these relationships. Peers nurture one another along the shared learning journey that the SOLE provides. As facilitator and designer, you are, most of all, in a reciprocal relationship with the other learners. This is the essence of being a peer, an interaction that respects what each of us brings to the experience.

## A review

> **Sugata Mitra**: It is great to see the thinking that has gone into taking the idea of a SOLE forward. To my mind, SOLEs are quite experimental at this time and efforts such as these will provide invaluable data. I look forward to this. I notice that most of the important design features of a SOLE are incorporated into the article. I repeat them anyway, just to emphasise:
>
> 1. Large, publicly visible displays are very important, this is what resulted in the surprising results in the hole in the wall experiments and subsequent SOLEs for children in England and elsewhere.
> 2. The absence of unnecessary people in the learning space, no matter who they are; parents,

teachers, principals, curious adults etc.

3. Free, undirected activity, conversation and movement.
4. A certain lack of order: I must emphasise that 'Self Organised', the way I use it does not mean 'organising of the self'. Instead it has a special meaning from the subject, Self Organising Systems, a part of Chaos Theory. The SOLE should be a space at the 'edge of chaos', thereby increasing the probability of the appearance of 'emergent order'.

## References

1. Preston, David (2014). Case Study: 5PH1NX (pp. 41–53, this volume).
2. About Sugata Mitra, on Wikispaces.
3. The SOLE Toolkit, on TED.com.
4. National Center for Universal Design for Learning, Universal Design for Learning Guidelines.
5. Sugata Mitra (2010). The child-driven education, TED.
6. Game-based Learning and Intrinsic Motivation by Kristi Mead.
7. Hidden Curriculum, on Wikipedia.
8. Transformed Learning Environment Analysis, by Jan Herder (on ScribD).
9. Elmasry, Sarah Khalil (2007). Integration Patterns of Learning Technologies. IRB# 05-295-06.
10. Curious: In-Forming singular/plural design, The Theories of Christopher Alexander.

11. Overwhelmed with Blog Tips? Hack Learning with Just In Time Information, on Wordstream.com.
12. Dichroic Filter, on Wikipedia.
13. UDL Guidelines on cast.org.
14. Active Learning Student Generated Syllabus, on theatre-prof.com.
15. User Generated Education Blog on wordpress.com.
16. Facebook as a Supplemental LMS, on telecentre.org.
17. Reciprocal Apprenticeship, on Star Wars Wikia.

# Part V

# Organizing a Learning Context

CHAPTER 13

# INTRODUCTION TO ORGANIZING CO-LEARNING

This section about organizing Co-Learning rests on the assumption that learning always happens in a context, whether this context is a structured "course" or a (potentially) less structured "learning space". For the moment we consider the following division:

- *Organizing Co-learning Contexts*
  - Courses ("linked to a timeline or syllabus")
  - Spaces ("not linked to a timeline or syllabus")

This section focuses on existing learning contexts and examines in detail how they have been "organized" by their (co-) creators. At a "meta-level" of development, we can talk about this parallel structure:

- *Building Co-learning Platforms*
  - Development trajectories (e.g. "design, implement, test, repeat")
  - Platform features (e.g. forums, wikis, ownership models, etc.)

A given learning environment with have both time-like and space-like features as well as both designed-for and un-planned features. A given learning platform will encourage certain types of engagement and impose certain constraints. The question for both "teachers" and "system designers" – as well as for learners – should be: *what features best support learning?*

The answer will depend on the learning task and available resources.

For example, nearly everyone agrees that the best way to learn a foreign language is through immersion. But not everyone who wants to learn, say, French, can afford to drop everything to go live in a French-speaking country. Thus, the space-like full immersion "treatment" is frequently sacrificed for course-like treatments (either via books, CDs, videos, or ongoing participation in semi-immersive discussion groups).

System designers are also faced with scarce resources: programmer time, software licensing concerns, availability of peer support, and so forth. While the ideal platform would (magically) come with solutions pre-built, a more realistic approach recognizes that problem solving always takes time and energy. The problem solving approach and associated "learning orientation" will also depend on the task and resources at hand. The following sections will develop this issue further through some specific case studies.

## Case Study 1: "Paragogy" and the After Action Review.

In our analysis of our experiences as course organizers at P2PU, we (Joe Corneli and Charlie Danoff) used the US Army's technique of After Action Review (AAR). To quote from our paper [2]:

> As the name indicates, the AAR is used to review training exercises. It is important to note that while one person typically plays the role of evaluator in such a review [...] the review itself happens among peers, and examines the operations of the unit as a whole.
>
> The four steps in an AAR are:
>
> 1. Review what was supposed to happen (training plans).
> 2. Establish what happened.
> 3. Determine what was right or wrong with what happened.

4. Determine how the task should be done differently the next time.

The stated purpose of the AAR is to "identify strengths and shortcomings in unit planning, preparation, and execution, and guide leaders to accept responsibility for shortcomings and produce a fix."

We combined the AAR with our paragogy principles –

1. Changing context as a decentered center.
2. Meta-learning as a font of knowledge.
3. Peers provide feedback that wouldn't be there otherwise.
4. Paragogy is distributed and nonlinear.
5. Realize the dream if you can, then wake up!

and went through steps 1-4 for each principle to look at how well it was implemented at P2PU. This process helped generate new policies that could be pursued further at P2PU or similar institutions. By presenteding our paper at the Open Knowledge Conference (OKCon), we were able to meet P2PU's executive director, Philipp Schmidt, as well as other highly-involved P2PU participants; our feedback may ultimately have contributed to shaping the development trajectory for P2PU.

In addition, we developed a strong prototype for constructive engagement with peer learning that we and others could deploy again. In other words, variants on the AAR and the paragogical principles could be incorporated into future learning contexts as platform features [3] or re-used in a design/administration/moderation approach [4]. For example, we also used the AAR to help structure our writing and subsequent work on paragogy.net.

## Case Study 2: Peeragogy, Year One.

We surveyed members of the Peeragogy community with questions similar to those used by Boud and Lee [1] and then identify strengths and shortcomings as we did with the AAR above.

## Questions

These were discussed, refined, and answered on an etherpad: revisions to the original set of questions, made by contributors, are marked in italics.

1. Who have you learned with or from in the Peeragogy project? *What are you doing to contribute to your peers' learning?*
2. How have you been learning during the project?
3. Who are your peers in this community, and why?
4. What were your expectations of participation in this project? *And, specifically, what did you (or do you) hope to learn through participation in this project?*
5. What actually happened during your participation in this project (so far)? *Have you been making progress on your learning goals (if any; see previous question) – or learned anything unexpected, but interesting?*
6. What is right or wrong with what happened (Alternatively: how would you assess the project to date?)
7. How might the task be done differently next time? (What's "missing" here that would create a "next time", *"sequel", or "continuation"?*)
8. *How would you like to use the Peeragogy handbook?*
9. *Finally, how might we change the questions, above, if we wanted to apply them in your peeragogical context?*

### Reflections on participants' answers

Some of the tensions highlighted in the answers are as follows:

1. *Slow formation of "peer" relationships.* There is a certain irony here: we are studying "peeragogy" and yet many respondents did not feel they were really getting to know one another "as peers", at least not yet. Those who did have a "team" or who knew one another from previous experiences, felt more peer-like in those relationships. Several re-

marked that they learned less from other individual participants and more from "the collective" or "from everyone". At the same time, some respondents had ambiguous feelings about naming individuals in the first question: "I felt like I was going to leave people out and that that means they would get a bad grade - ha!" One criterion for being a peer was to have built something together, so by this criterion, it stands to reason that we would only slowly become peers through this project.

2. *"Co-learning", "co-teaching", "co-producing"?* One respondent wrote: "I am learning about peeragogy, but I think I'm failing [to be] a good peeragogue. I remember that Howard [once] told us that the most important thing is that you should be responsible not only for your own learning but for your peers' learning. [...] So the question is, are we learning from others by ourselves or are we [...] helping others to learn?" Another wrote: "To my surprise I realized I could contribute organizationally with reviews, etc. And that I could provide some content around PLNs and group process. Trying to be a catalyst to a sense of forward movement and esprit de corps."

3. *Weak structure at the outset, versus a more "flexible" approach.* One respondent wrote: "I definitely think I do better when presented with a framework or scaffold to use for participation or content development. [...] (But perhaps it is just that I'm used to the old way of doing things)." Yet, the same person wrote: "I am interested in [the] applicability [of pæragogy] to new models for entrepreneurship enabling less structured aggregation of participants in new undertakings, freed of the requirement or need for an entrepreneurial visionary/source/point person/proprietor." There is a sense that some confusion, particularly at the beginning, may be typical for peeragogy. With hindsight, one proposed "solution" would be to "have had a small group of people as a cadre that had met and brainstormed before the

first live session [...] tasked [with] roles [and] on the same page".

4. *Technological concerns.* There were quite a variety, perhaps mainly to do with the question: how might a (different) platform handle the tension between "conversations" and "content production"? For example, will Wordpress help us "bring in" new contributors, or would it be better to use an open wiki? Another respondent noted the utility for many readers of a take-away PDF version. The site (peeragogy.org) should be "[a] place for people to share, comment, mentor and co-learn together in an ongoing fashion."

5. *Sample size.* Note that answers are still trickling in. How should we interpret the response rate? Perhaps what matters is that we are getting "enough" responses to make an analysis. One respondent proposed asking questions in a more ongoing fashion, e.g., asking people who are leaving: "What made you want to quit the project?"

## Discussion

> **Lisewski and Joyce**: In recent years, the tools, knowledge base and discourse of the learning technology profession has been bolstered by the appearance of conceptual paradigms such as the 'five stage e-moderating model' and the new mantra of 'communities of practice'. This paper will argue that, although these frameworks are useful in informing and guiding learning technology practice, there are inherent dangers in them becoming too dominant a discourse. [5]

Instead of a grand narrative, Peeragogy is a growing collection of case studies and descriptive patterns. As we share our experiences and make needed adaptations, our techniques for doing peer learning and peer production become more robust. Based on the experiences described above, here are a few things people may want to try out in future projects:

- "Icebreaking" techniques or a "buddy system"; continual refactoring into teams.
- Maintain a process diagram that can be used to "triage" new ideas and effort.
- Prefer the "good" to the "best", but make improvements at the platform level as needed.
- Gathering some information from everyone who joins, and, if possible, everyone who leaves.

## References

1. Boud, D. and Lee, A. (2005). 'Peer learning' as pedagogic discourse for research education. *Studies in Higher Education*, 30(5):501–516.
2. Joseph Corneli and Charles Jeffrey Danoff, Paragogy, in Sebastian Hellmann, Philipp Frischmuth, Sören Auer, and Daniel Dietrich (eds.), *Proceedings of the 6th Open Knowledge Conference, Berlin, Germany, June 30 & July 1, 2011*,
3. Joseph Corneli and Alexander Mikroyannidis (2011). Personalised and Peer-Supported Learning: The Peer-to-Peer Learning Environment (P2PLE), *Digital Education Review*, 20.
4. Joseph Corneli, Paragogical Praxis, *E-Learning and Digital Media* (ISSN 2042-7530), Volume 9, Number 3, 2012
5. Lisewski, B., and P. Joyce (2003). Examining the Five Stage e-Moderating Model: Designed and Emergent Practice in the Learning Technology Profession, *Association for Learning Technology Journal*, 11, 55-66.

CHAPTER 14

# ADDING STRUCTURE WITH ACTIVITIES

In the introduction to "Organizing a Learning Context", we remarked that a "learning space" is *only potentially* less structured than a "course". For example, a library tends to be highly structured, with quiet rooms for reading, protocols for checking out books, a cataloging and shelving system that allows people to find what they are looking for, as well as rules that deter vandalism and theft. (Digital libraries don't need to play by all the same rules, but are still structured.)

But more structure does not always lead to better learning. In a 2010 Forbes article titled, "The Classroom in 2020," George Kembel describes a future in which "Tidy lectures will be supplanted by messy real-world challenges." The Stanford School of Design, (or "d.school" – which Kemble co-founded and currently directs) is already well-known for its open collaborative spaces, abundant supply of Post-It notes and markers, and improvisational brainstorm activities – almost the opposite of traditional lecture-based learning.

One "unexpected benefit" of dealing with real-world challenges is that we can change our approach as we go. This is how it works in peer learning: peers can decide on different structures not just once (say, at the beginning of a course), but throughout the duration of their time together. This way, they are never "stuck" with existing structures, whether they be messy or clean. At least... that's the ideal.

In practice, "bottlenecks" frequently arise. For example, in a digital library context, there may be bottlenecks having to do with software development, organizational resources, community good will, or access to funding – and probably all of the above. In a didactic context, it may be as simple as one person knowing something that others do not.

While we can't eliminate scarcity in one stroke, we can design activities for peer learning that are "scarcity aware" and that help us move in the direction of adaptive learning structures.

## Planning Peer Learning Activities

We begin with two simple questions:

- How do we select an appropriate learning activity?
- How do we go about creating a learning activity if we don't find an existing one?

"Planning a learning activity" should mean planning an *effective* learning activity, and in particular that means something that people can and will engage with. In short, an appropriate learning activity may be one that you already do! At the very least, current activities can provide a "seed" for even more effective ones.

But when entering unfamiliar territory, it can be difficult to know where to begin. And remember the bottlenecks mentioned above? When you run into difficulty, ask yourself: why is this hard? You might try adapting Zed Shaw's task-management trick, and make a list of limiting factors, obstacles, etc., then cross off those which you can find a strategy to deal with (add an annotation as to why). For example, you might decide to overcome your lack of knowledge in some area by hiring a tutor or expert consultant, or by putting in the hours learning things the hard way (Zed would particularly approve of this choice). If you can't find a strategy to deal with some issue, presumably you can table it, at least for a while.

Strategic thinking like this works well for one person. What about when you're planning activities for someone else? Here you have to be careful: remember, this is peer learning, not traditional "teaching" or "curriculum design". The first rule of thumb for *peer learning* is: don't plan activities for others unless you plan to to take part as a fully engaged participant. Otherwise, you might be more interested in the literature on *collaborative learning*, which has often been deployed to good effect within a standard pedagogical context (see e.g. Bruffee [1]). In a peer learning setting, everyone will have something to say about "what do you need to do" and "why is it hard," and everyone is likely to be interested in everyone else's answer as well as their own.

Furthermore, different participants will be doing different things, and these will "hard" for different reasons. Part of *your* job is to try to make sure all of the relevant roles are covered by someone and to try to make sure that they're getting enough support.

## One scenario: building activities for the Peeragogy Handbook

Adding a bunch of activities to the handbook won't solve all of our usability issues, but more activities would help. We can think about each article or section from this perspective:

1. When looking at this piece of text, what type of knowledge are we (and the reader) trying to gain? Technical skills, or abstract skills? What's the point?
2. What's difficult here? What might be difficult for someone else?
3. What learning activity recipes or models might be appropriate? (See e.g. [2], [3].)
4. What customizations do we need for this particular application?

### As a quick example: designing a learning activity for the current page

1. *We want to be able to come up with effective learning activities to accompany a "how to" article for peer learners*

2. *It might be difficult to "unplug" from all the reading and writing that we're habituated to doing.*

3. *But there are lots and lots of ways to learn.*

4. *Therefore, the proposed handbook activity is to simply step away from the handbook for a while.*

   **Look for some examples of peer learning in every-day life. When you've gained an insight about peer learning from your own experience, come back and create a related activity to accompany another hand-book page!**

## References

1. Bruffee, Kenneth A. (1984). "Collaborative learning and the conversation of mankind." *College English* 46.7, 635-652
2. KS ToolKit from kstoolkit.org.
3. Designing Effective and Innovative Sources (particularly the section on "Teaching Strategies for Actively Engaging Students in the Classroom")

CHAPTER 15

# THE STUDENT AUTHORED SYLLABUS

Suz Burroughs

In either formal learning, informal learning or models which transition between the two, there are many opportunities for learners to co-create the syllabus and/or outline their own course of action. The *sage on the stage* of formal instruction must become at the most *a guide on the side* who acts as a coach appearing only when needed rather than as a lecturer who determines the content that the learners need to master. In the following inspirational but certainly not prescriptive examples, we will focus on co-learning methods drawn from a Social Constructivist perspective, which fits nicely here.

We offer a few examples below to show a range of learner centered approaches. They all are based on co-learners hosting each other for one of a number of digestible topics in the larger subject area or domain that the group formed in order to explore. This can take place across a number of media and timelines.

The following methods will result in each co-learner gaining deep knowledge in a specific topic and moderate knowledge across several topics. The unique joy of this approach is that no two cohorts will ever be the same. The content will always be fresh, relevant, and changing. A group can even reconvene with slightly or dramatically different topics over and over using the same underlying process.

The appropriateness of the learner-created syllabus technique depends on two factors: 1) the involvement of experts in the group and 2) the level of proficiency of the group. In general, novices who may or may not have a deep interest in the subject matter benefit from more structure and experts who point to key concepts and texts. An example of this is the university survey course for first or second year students who, we assume, need more guidance as they enter the subject matter. Graduate seminars are generally much more fluid, open dialogues between motivated experts require little structure or guidance.

We also need effective methods for groups which contain novices, experts, and everyone in between. In groups with a wide range of expertise, it is important that each co-learner chooses to focus their deep inquiry on a topic that they are less familiar with. This will *even out* the expertise level across the cohort as well as ensure that a co-learner is neither bored nor dominating the dialogue.

## 3 example designs to structure the learning

### Weekly topics structure

One way to structure the course is to have each co-learner host a topic each week. Perhaps multiple students host their topics in the same week. This progression provides a rotation of presentations and activities to support the entire group in engaging with the topics and challenges to the thinking of the presenters in a constructive and respectful manner.

> *Pro:* co-learners have discrete timelines and manageable chunks of responsibility.
>
> *Con:* the format may become disjointed, and the depth of inquiry will likely be somewhat shallow.

### Milestone based structure

In this structure, each co-learner host their topics in parallel with similar activities and milestones that the whole group moves through together. Milestones can be set for a certain date, or the group can *unlock* their next milestone whenever all participants have completed the previous milestone. This second milestone timeline can be great for informal groups where participation levels may vary from week to week due to external factors, and the sense of responsibility and game-like levels can be motivating for many co-learners.

Each co-learner may start with a post of less than 500 words introducing the topic on a superficial level. When everyone has done this, the group might move on to posting questions to the post authors. Then, there may be a summary post of the activity so far with critical recommendations or insights.

> *Pro:* co- learners have more time to digest a topic, formulate a complex schema, and generate deeper questions.
>
> *Con:* it will be a few weeks before the topic level schema can form into a broader understanding of the subject matter or domain (seeing the big picture takes longer).

### Relay learning structure.

This is similar to the milestone structure. However, co-learners rotate topics. If one learner posts an introductory write-up on a topic the first cycle, they may be researching questions on another topic in the next cycle, posting a summary in a third, and then posting a summary on their original topic in the fourth.

> *Pro:* co-learners can experience responsibility for several topics.
>
> *Con:* co-learners may receive a topic that is poorly researched or otherwise neglected.

## Content

### A vast number of topics

Within a subject of mutual interest to a group, there are a considerable number of topics or questions. What is important is that each co-learner can take responsibility for a reasonably narrow area given the duration of the course or the timeline of the group. Areas that are too broad will result in a very superficial understanding, and areas that are too narrow will result in a dull experience. For example, in marine biology, topics such as "the intertidal zone" may be too broad for a course cycle of a few weeks. Narrowing to one species may be too specific for a course over a few months.

### Learner generated topics

Most cohorts will have some knowledge of the shared area of interest or an adjacent area. It is a good idea to respect the knowledge and experience that each member of the group brings to the table. A facilitator or coordinator may generate a list of potential topic areas, setting an example of the scale of a topic. We suggest that the participants in the group are also polled for additions to the list. In large courses, sending out a Google Form via email can be an effective way to get a quick list with a high response rate.

### Expert informed topics

If there is no expert facilitator in the group, we suggest that the cohort begin their journey with a few interviews of experts to uncover what the main buzz words and areas of focus might be. One way to locate this type of expert help is through contacting authors in the subject matter on social networks, reviewing their posts for relevance, and reaching out with the request.

We recommend two people interview the expert over video chat, for example in a Hangout. One person conducts the interview, and one person takes notes and watches the time. We strongly suggest that the interview be outlined ahead of time:

> *Warm up*: Who are you, what are your goals, and why do you think this interview will help?
>
> *Foundational questions*: Ask a few questions that might elicit short answers to build rapport and get your interviewee talking.
>
> *Inquiry*: What people say and what they do can often be very different. Ask about topics required for mastery of the subject matter (e.g. What are the areas

someone would need to know about to be considered proficient in this subject?). Also, ask questions that require storytelling. Avoid superlative or close-ended questions.

*Wrap up*: Thank the interviewee for his or her time, and be sure to follow up by sharing both what you learned and what you accomplished because he or she helped you.

## Shared goals and group norms

### Choosing useful outputs

Getting together for the sake of sharing what you know in an informal way can be fairly straightforward and somewhat useful. Most groups find that a common purpose and output that are explicitly defined and documented help to engage, motivate, and drive the group. For the examples above, the group may decide to create a blog with posts on the various topics or create a wiki where they can share their insights. Other outputs can include community service projects, business proposals, recommendations to senior management or administration, new products, and more. The key is to go beyond sharing for sharing sake and move toward an output that will be of use beyond the co-learning group. This activity is best described in Connectivist theory as the special case of networked learning where we find evidence of learning in collective action and/or behavioral change in groups rather than a psychological or neurological process in individuals.

### Group cohesion (a.k.a. the rules of the road)

One challenge of this kind of collaboration is that each group will need to decide on norms, acceptable practices and behaviors. Culturally diverse groups in particular may run into communication or other issues unless there is a way to create shared expectations and communicate preferences.

One way to do this is with a team charter. This is a living document where the initial rules of engagement can live for reference. The group may add or edit this document over time based on experience, and that is a welcome thing! This documentation is a huge asset for new members joining the group who want to contribute quickly and effectively. Any co-editing word processing program will work, but we strongly recommend something that can be edited simultaneously and that lives in the cloud. (Google Docs is convenient because you can also embed your Charter into another site.)

Try starting with the following three sections, and allow some time for the group to co-edit and negotiate the document between icebreakers and kicking off the official learning process.

> *Mission:* Why are you forming the group? What do you want to accomplish together?
>
> *Norms:* Use netiquette? No flaming? Post your vacation days to a shared calendar? Cultural norms?
>
> *Members:* It is useful to include a photo and a link to a public profile such as Twitter, Google+ or Facebook.

## Assessments and feedback loops

### Co-authored assessment rubrics

Tests. Quizzes. Exams. How can the co-learning group assess their performance?

These types of courses benefit from an approach similar to coaching. Set goals as individuals and a group in the beginning, define what success looks like, outline steps that are needed to achieve the goal, check in on the goal progress periodically, and assess the results at the end of the course against the goal criteria. Goals may include domain expertise, a business outcome, a paper demonstrating mastery, a co-created resource, or even the quality of collaboration and adherence to shared group norms.

## Learner created assessments

Another effective way to create an assessment is to decide on an individual or group output and create a peer assessment rubric based on the goals of the individual or group.

One way to create a rubric is to spend some time defining the qualities you want your output to have based on positive examples. Perhaps a group wants to create a blog. Each person on the team may identify the qualities of a great blog post based on examples that they admire. They can use that example to create a criteria for assessment of co-learner authored blog posts. We recommend that the criteria have a 0 to 5 point scale with 0 being non-existent and 5 being superb. Writing a few indicators in the 1, 3, and 5 columns helps to calibrate reviewers.

Create a shared document, perhaps starting with a list of criteria. Collapse similar criteria into one item, and create the indicators or definitions of 1, 3, and 5 point performance. Agree on the rubric, and decide on how the co-learners will be assigned assessment duties. WIll everyone review at least two others? Will each co-learner product need at least 3 reviewers before it goes live? Will you use a spreadsheet or a form to collect the assessments?

In a university setting, the instructor of record may wish to approve a peer assessment rubric, and it is sometimes a good idea to have a few outside experts give feedback on criteria that the group may have missed.

## Outside assessments

It is possible that an instructor of record or similar authority will create the assessment for performance. In these cases, it is crucial that the co-learners have access to the grading rubric ahead of time so that they can ensure their activities and timeline will meet any requirements. In this case, it may be possible to require that the co-learners self-organize entirely, or there may be intermediary assignments such as the charter, project plan or literary review.

## Cyclical use of these models

### So much more to learn

As mentioned above, the joy of this type of learning is that no two groups will ever do it the same. Their process, goals, and outcomes can all be unique. As designers and facilitators of this type of learning environment, we can say it is a wild ride! Each class is exciting, refreshing, and on trend. The co-learners become our teachers.

If a group generates more topics than it is possible to cover at one time given the number of group members or if a group has plans to continue indefinitely, it is always possible to set up a system where potential topics are collected at all times. These unexplored topics can be harvested for use in another learning cycle, continuing until the group achieves comprehensive mastery.

## Risks

This format is not without its own unique pitfalls: some challenges are learner disorientation or frustration in a new learning structure with ambiguous expectations and uneven participation. Some groups simply never gel, and we do not know why they have failed to achieve the cohesion required to move forward. Other groups are the exact opposite. Here are a few risks to consider if you would like to try the methods suggested here and how to mitigate them.

> *Uneven expertise:* Ask co-learners to be responsible for topics that are new to them.
>
> *Uneven participation and cohesion:* Ask co-learners what they want to do to motivate the group rather than imposing your own ideas.
>
> *Experts/facilitators that kill the conversation:* In the charter or other documentation, explicitly state that the purpose of the discussion is to further the conversation, and encourage experts to allow others to ex-

plore their own thinking by asking probing (not leading) questions.

*Ambiguous goals:* Encourage the group to document their mission and what they will do as a team. This can change over time, but it is best to start out with a clear purpose.

## Conclusion

Make mistakes. Correct course. Invite new perspectives. Create a structure that everyone can work with. Change it when it breaks. Most of all, have fun!

CHAPTER 16

# CASE STUDY: COLLABORATIVE EXPLORATIONS

PETER TAYLOR & TERYL CARTWRIGHT

## Part I (Peter).

Collaborative Exploration invites participants to shape their own directions of inquiry and develop their skills as investigators and teachers (in the broadest sense of the word). The basic mode of a Collaborative Exploration centers on interactions over a delimited period of time in small groups. Engagement takes place either online, for instance via Google+, or face-to-face. The aim is to create an experience of re-engagement with oneself as an avid learner and inquirer. This section combines practical information about how to run Collaborative Explorations as well as ideas and questions about how to make sense of what happens in them. A companion entry conveys one participant's experience with several Collaborative Explorations (hereafter, "CE").

### Overview and contrast to cMOOCs

The tangible goal of any CE is to develop contributions to the topic defined by the "case", which is written by the host or originator of the CE in advance, and which is intended to be broad and thought-provoking (some examples are given below). We aim for a parallel experiential goal, which is that we hope participants will be impressed at how much can be learned with a small commitment of time using this structure. The standard model for an online CE is to have four sessions spaced one week apart, in which the same small group interacts in real time via the internet, for an hour per session. Participants are asked to spend at least 90 minutes between sessions on self-directed inquiry into the case, and to share their inquiries-in-progress with their small group and a wider community. Reflection typically involves shifts in participants' definition of what they want to find out and how. Any participants wondering how to define a meaningful and useful line of inquiry are encouraged to review the scenario for the CE, any associated materials, posts from other participants, and think about what they would like to learn more about or dig deeper into. Everyone is left, in the end, to judge for themselves whether what interests them is meaningful and useful. During the live sessions, participants can expect to do a lot of listening, starting off in the first session with autobiographical stories that make it easier to trust and take risks with whoever has joined that CE, and a lot of writing to gather their thoughts, sometimes privately, sometimes shared. There is no assumption that participants will pursue the case beyond the limited duration of the CE. This said, the tools and processes that the CE employs for purposes of inquiry, dialogue, reflection, and collaboration are designed to be readily learned by participants, and to translate well into other settings – for instance, where they can be used to support the inquiries of others. In short, online CEs are moderate-sized open online collaborative learning. It remains to be seen whether the CE "movement" will attract enough participants to scale up to multiple learning communities around any given scenario, each hosted by a different person and running independently. A MOOC (massive open online course) seeks to get masses of people registered, knowing that a tiny fraction will complete it, while CE best practices focus on establishing effective learning in small online communities, and then potentially scale up from there by multiplying out. CEs aim to address the needs of online learners who want to:

- dig deeper, make "thicker" connections with other learners
- connect topics with their own interests
- participate for short periods of time
- learn without needing credits or badges

Currently, even the most high-profile MOOCs do not appear to be conducive to deep or thick inquiry. For example, while link-sharing is typical in "connectivist" or "cMOOCs", annotation and discussion of the contents is less common. By contrast, CEs are structured to elicit participants' thoughtful reflections and syntheses. The use of the internet for CEs, in contrast, is guided by two principles of online education (Taylor 2007).

- Use computers first and foremost to teach or learn things that are difficult to teach or learn with pedagogical approaches that are not based on computers
- Model computer use, at least initially, on known best practices for teaching/learning without computers.

Thus, CEs bring in participants from a distance, make rapid connections with informants or discussants outside the course, and contribute to evolving guides to materials and resources. At the same time, participants benefit from the support of instructors/facilitators and peers who they can trust, and integrate what they learn with their own personal, pedagogical, and professional development.

## Example scenarios or "cases"

### Connectivist MOOCs: Learning and collaboration, possibilities and limitations

The core faculty member of a graduate program at a public urban university wants help as they decide how to contribute to efforts at the university program to promote open digital education. It is clear that the emphasis will not be on xMOOCs, i.e., those designed for transmission of established knowledge, but on cMOOCs. In other words, the plan is to emphasize connectivist learning and community development emerges around, but may extend well beyond, the materials provided by the MOOC hosts (Morrison 2013; Taylor 2013). What is not yet clear about is just how learning works in cMOOCs. What are the possibilities and limitations of this educational strategy? How do they bear on themes like creativity, community, collaboration, and openness? The program is especially interested in anticipating any undesirable consequences...

### Science and policy that would improve responses to extreme climatic events

Recent and historical climate-related events shed light on the social impact of emergency plans, investment in and maintenance of infrastructure, as well as investment in reconstruction. Policy makers, from the local level up, can learn from the experiences of others and prepare for future crises. The question for this case is how to get political authorities and political groups—which might be anywhere from the town level to the international, from the elected to the voluntary—interested in learning about how best to respond to extreme climatic events. Changes might take place at the level of policy, budget, organization, and so on. It should even be possible to engage people who do not buy into the idea of human-induced climate change—after all, whatever the cause, extreme climatic events have to be dealt with....

## The structure

Independent of the topic, we've found the following common structure useful for our online CEs. *Before the first live session*: Participants review the scenario, the expectations and mechanics, join a special-purpose Google+ community and get set up technically for the hangouts.

**Session 1**: *Participants getting to know each other.* After freewriting to clarify thoughts and hopes, followed by a quick check-in, participants take 5 minutes each to tell the story of how they came to be a person who would be interested to participate in a Collaborative Exploration on the scenario. Other participants note connections with the speaker and possible ways to extend their interests, sharing these using an online form.

*Between-session work*: Spend at least 90 minutes on inquiries related to the case, posting about this to google+ community for the CE, and reviewing the posts of others.

**Session 2**: *Clarify thinking and inquiries.* Freewriting on one's thoughts about the case, followed by a check-in, then turn-taking "dialogue process" to clarify what participants are thinking about their inquiries into the case. Session finishes with gathering and sharing thoughts using an online form.

*Between-session work*: Spend at least 90 minutes (a) on inquiries related to the case and (b) preparing a work-in-progress presentation.

**Session 3**: *Work-in-progress presentations.* 5 minutes for each participant, with "plus-delta" feedback given by everyone on each presentation.

*Between-session work*: Digest the feedback on one's presentation and revise it into a self-standing product (i.e., one understandable without spoken narration).

**Session 4**: *Taking Stock.* Use same format as for session 2 to explore participants' thinking about (a) how the Collaborative Exploration contributed to the topic (the tangible goal) and to the experiential goal, as well as (b) how to extend what has emerged during the CE.

*After session 4 (optional)*: Participants share on a public Google+ community not only the products they have prepared, but also reflections on the Collaborative Exploration process.

## How to make sense of what happens in CEs

(Re-)engagement with oneself as an avid learner and inquirer in CEs is made possible by the combination of:

- Processes and tools used for inquiry, dialogue, reflection, and collaboration;
- Connections made among the diverse participants who bring to bear diverse interests, skills, knowledge, experience, and aspirations; and

- Contributions from the participants to the topics laid out in scenarios.

The hope is that through experiencing a (re-)engagement with learning, participants will subsequently transfer experience with this triad into their own inquiries and teaching-learning interactions, the ways that they support inquiries of others; other practices of critical intellectual exchange and cooperation; and that they will be more prepared to challenge the barriers to learning that are often associated with expertise, location, time, gender, race, class, or age.

## Acknowledgements

The comments of Jeremy Szteiter and the contributions of the participants of the 2013 Collaborative Explorations have helped in the preparation of this article.

# Part II (Teryl).

As a May graduate of the Master's program in Critical and Creative Thinking (CCT) at UMass Boston, I owe my gratitude to Professors Peter Taylor and Jeremy Szteiter for inviting me to informally continue my education less than a month later. It is a tribute to them that I would then take four consecutive CEs without stopping. They can best share how to run a CE, but as a "student," it is how to creatively take a CE that inspires what I'd like to share.

**June 2013 CE: Scaffolding Creative Learning** I was grateful participants took the time to post links and ideas to support my inquiries, yet something else intrigued me about the potential of Collaborative Exploration. Luanne Witkowski, an artist and one of the CCT instructors, took our ideas and made a diagram incorporating our scaffolding concepts together; she changed her own original drawing to include all of ours. I wanted to pay forward and back my learning too, so I combined the ideas of all the participants, adapted and taught a lesson outside the CE and then shared the results. From this jumping into someone else's scaffolding, I went into even more experimental learning in the next CE.

**July 2013 CE: Design in Critical Thinking** In a second CE, I took the title literally and developed a design IN critical thinking. To try out my triangle tangent thinking model, during a lesson on leadership in church, I suddenly stopped teaching a classroom of older professional adults halfway in and asked them to participate in "design as you go" curriculum—by taking over the class. Since I wanted to be fair, along with my lesson outline I had already given them a supposed "icebreaker" activity that they could teach from, although they also had the option of my continued teaching. Results? My triangle drawing works as a lesson plan; the class took the tangent, but surprisingly, I wasn't just relegated to moderator, it became a true co-facilitation,a model of change at the midpoint for both the individual and community in the choices and direction.

**September 2013 CE: Everyone Can Think Creatively** This CE had to be commended for its participants humoring my project and allowing the exploration of testing a CE itself. Was it possible to be a Creative Failure in a Creativity CE? To evaluate "Creative Failure in a Creativity CE," I used a simple test. If creative success (unknowingly given by my CE community) was a product both "novel AND useful," any post without a comment was a failure ("not useful") to my readers. Any post that a reader commented was similar to something else already done was "useful," but not novel. Failure had me posting again. Did I mention what nice people these were when they didn't know what I was doing? It would have been easy for them to ignore my continued posting, yet the community of a CE cannot be praised enough. They were supportive of me and finding academic colleagues who have a sense of humor is mercifully not novel, but extremely useful in this experience.

**October 2013 CE: Stories to Scaffold Creative Learning** In this CE I gave myself the challenge of indirect teaching. Could I be a story "shower", not teller? I took concepts important to me about teaching with story, yet also tried to leave space for others' interpretations. Ironically, in some ways creative failure continued—again I was not as helpful as I had wished. This CE also had a twist—no hero stories allowed, so my creative and personal stories had to be ambiguous or use other connecting structures based on the participants' preferences. It was interesting which stories worked best—fiction worked more with humor, real experience worked if I shared about someone other than myself and other kinds worked with visuals.Collaborative Explorations provide a safe space for the joint learning and teaching to occur. The diversity blends well into a community that is curious, courageous and creative. Although I have my M.A. as the first completely online CCT student, I found almost a face-to-face learning "feel" in their deeply connected CE community as well. It does require time, openness and commitment to each other during the intense focus together on a topic. Yet seeing where the participant-directed 'design as you go' curriculum ends up is worth investing in and sharing with others. After all, there are many other ways still out there to try out CEs.

**Postscript** I also ran a CE for the Susquehanna Conference of the UMC for 10 days, working with a group of professionals exploring a call into ordained ministry. Going in cold, I had to work harder to do community building without the Google hangout meetings and recommend their inclusion to increase the comfort level and participation of the group members.

## Resources

Further examples of CE scenarios can be viewed at

`http://cct.wikispaces.com/CEt.`

Recommended readings below convey some of the sources for the CE processes. Ideas about possible extensions of CEs can be viewed in the full prospectus at

`http://cct.wikispaces.com/CEp.`

## References

1. Morrison, D. (2013). "A tale of two MOOCs @ Coursera: Divided by pedagogy".
2. Taylor, P. J. (2007) "Guidelines for ensuring that educational technologies are used only when there is significant pedagogical benefit," International Journal of Arts and Sciences, 2 (1): 26-29, 2007 (adapted from http://bit.ly/etguide).
3. Taylor, P. J. (2013). "Supporting change in creative learning".

## Recommended Reading

1. Paley, V. G. (1997). The Girl with the Brown Crayon. Cambridge, MA, Harvard University Press.
2. Paley, V.G. (2010). The Boy on the Beach: Building Community by Play. Chicago, University of Chicago Press.
3. Taylor, P. J. and J. Szteiter (2012). Taking Yourself Seriously: Processes of Research and Engagement Arlington, MA, The Pumping Station.
4. White, M. (2011). Narrative Practice: Continuing the Conversation. New York, Norton.

# Part VI

# Cooperation

CHAPTER 17

# INTRODUCTION TO COOPERATION: CO-FACILITATION

Maria Arenas & Charlie Danoff

Facilitation is a process of helping groups work cooperatively and effectively. Facilitation can be particularly helpful for individuals who, based on a certain level of insecurity or inexperience, tend to lurk rather than participate. At the same time, it in peeragogy, a facilitator isn't necessarily an "authority": rather, facilitation work is done in service to the group and the group dialogue and process. For example, a facilitator may simply "hold space" for the group, by setting up a meeting or a regular series of discussions.

## Co-facilitating in peer-to-peer learning

Co-facilitation can be found in collaborations between two or more people who need each other to complete a task, for example, learn about a given subject, author a technical report, solve a problem, or conduct research Dee Fink writes that "in this process, there has to be some kind of change in the learner. No change, no learning" [1]. Significant learning requires that there be some kind of lasting change that is important in terms of the learner's life; in peeragogy, one way to measure the effectiveness of co-facilitation is to look for a change in the peer group.

Co-facilitation roles can be found in groups/teams like basketball, health, Alcoholics Anonymous, spiritual groups, etc. For example, self-help groups are composed of people who gather to share common problems and experiences associated with a particular problem, condition, illness, or personal circumstance. There are some further commonalities across different settings. Commenting on the work of Carl Rogers:

> **Godfrey Barrett-Lennard**: The educational situation which most effectively promotes significant learning is one in which (1) threat to the self of the learner is reduced a minimum, and (2) differentiated perception of the field of experience is facilitated. [2]

Part of the facilitator's role is to create a safe place for learning to take place; but they should also challenge the participants.

> **John Heron**: Too much hierarchical control, and participants become passive and dependent or hostile and resistant. They wane in self-direction, which is the core of all learning. Too much cooperative guidance may degenerate into a subtle kind of nurturing oppression, and may deny the group the benefits of totally autonomous learning. Too much autonomy for participants and laissez-faire on your part, and they may wallow in ignorance, misconception, and chaos. [3]

## Co-facilitating discussion forums

If peers are preparing a forum discussion, here are some ideas from "The Community Tool Box", that can be helpful as guidelines:

- Explain the importance of collaborative group work and make it a requirement.
- Establish how you will communicate in the forum.
- Be aware of mutual blind spots in facilitating and observing others.
- Watch out for different rhythms of intervention.

## Co-facilitating wiki workflows

A good place to begin for any group of co-facilitators working with a wiki are Wikipedia's famous "5 Pillars."

- Wikipedia is an encyclopedia.
- Wikipedia writes articles from a neutral point-of-view.
- Wikipedia is free content that anyone can edit, use, modify, and distribute.
- Editors should interact with each other in a respectful and civil manner.
- Wikipedia does not have firm rules.

## Co-facilitating live sessions

Learning experiences in live sessions are described in the article Learning Re-imagined: Participatory, Peer, Global, Online by Howard Rheingold, and many of these points are revisited in the handbook section on real-time tools. But we want to emphasize one point here:

> **Howard Rheingold**: Remember you came together with your peers to accomplish something, not to discuss an agenda or play with online tools; keep everything as easily accessible as possible to ensure you realize your goals.

## References

1. Fink, L. D (2003). *Creating significant learning experiences: An integrated approach to designing college courses.* John Wiley & Sons.
2. Barrett-Lennard, G. T. (1998). *Carl Rogers' Helping System: Journey & Substance.* Sage.
3. Heron, J. (1999). *The complete facilitator's handbook.* London: Kogan Page.

CHAPTER 18

# THE WORKSCAPE, A LEARNING PLATFORM FOR CORPORATIONS

Jay Cross

Cultivating a results-oriented peer-learning program in a corporate learning ecosystem involves a few tweaks of the approach and tools we discussed in relation to more open, diverse networks.

## The Workscape, a platform for learning

Formal learning takes place in classrooms; informal learning happens in *workscapes.* A workscape is a learning ecology. As the environment of learning, a workscape includes the workplace. In fact, a workscape has no boundaries. No two workscapes are alike. Your workscape may include being coached on giving effective presentations, calling the help desk for an explanation, and researching an industry on the Net. My workscape could include participating in a community of field technicians, looking things up on a search engine, and living in France for three months. Developing a platform to support informal learning is analogous to landscaping a garden. A major component of informal learning is natural learning, the notion of treating people as organisms in nature. The people are free-range learners. Our role is to protect their environment, provide nutrients for growth, and let nature take its course. A landscape designer's goal is to conceptualize a harmonious, unified, pleasing garden that makes the most of the site at hand. A workscape designer's goal is to create a learning environment that increases the organization's longevity and health and the individual's happiness and well-being. Gardeners don't control plants; managers don't control people. Gardeners and managers have influence but not absolute authority. They can't makea plant fit into the landscape or a person fit into a team. In an ideal Workscape, workers can easily find the people and information they need, learning is fluid and new ideas flow freely, corporate citizens live and work by the organization's values, people know the best way to get things done, workers spend more time creating value than handling exceptions, and everyone finds their work challenging and fulfilling.

## The technical infrastructure of the Workscape

When an organization is improving its Workscape, looking at consumer applications is a good way to think about what's required. Ask net-savvy younger workers how they would like to learn new skills, and they bring up the features they enjoy in other services:

- Personalize my experience and make recommendations, like Amazon.
- Make it easy for me to connect with friends, like Facebook.
- Keep me in touch with colleagues and associates in other companies, as on LinkedIn.
- Persistent reputations, as at eBay, so you can trust who you're collaborating with.
- Multiple access options, like a bank that offers access by ATM, the Web, phone, or human tellers.
- Don't overload me. Let me learn from YouTube, an FAQ, or linking to an expert.
- Show me what's hot, like Reddit, Digg, MetaFilter, or Fark do.
- Give me single sign-on, like using my Facebook profile to access multiple applications.
- Let me choose and subscribe to streams of information I'm interested in, like BoingBoing, LifeHacker or Huffpost.
- Provide a single, simple, all-in-one interface, like that provided by Google for search.

- Help me learn from a community of kindred spirits, like SlashDot, Reddit, and MetaFilter.
- Give me a way to voice my opinions and show my personality, as on my blog.
- Show me what others are interested in, as with social bookmarks like Diigo and Delicious.
- Make it easy to share photos and video, as on Flickr and YouTube.
- Leverage "the wisdom of crowds," as when I pose a question to my followers on Twitter or Facebook.
- Enable users to rate content, like "Favoriting" an item on Facebook or +!ing is on Google or YouTube.

Some of those consumer applications are simple to replicate in-house. Others are not. You can't afford to replicate Facebook or Google behind your firewall. That said, there are lots of applications you can implement at reasonable cost. Be skeptical if your collaborative infrastructure that doesn't include these minimal functions:

**Profiles** - for locating and contacting people with the right skills and background. Profile should contain photo, position, location, email address, expertise (tagged so it's searchable). IBM's Blue Pages profiles include how to reach you (noting whether you're online now), reporting chain (boss, boss's boss, etc.), link to your blog and bookmarks, people in your network, links to documents you frequently share, members of your network.

**Activity stream** - for monitoring the organization pulse in real time, sharing what you're doing, being referred to useful information, asking for help, accelerating the flow of news and information, and keeping up with change

**Wikis** - for writing collaboratively, eliminating multiple versions of documents, keeping information out in the open, eliminating unnecessary email, and sharing responsibility for updates and error correction

**Virtual meetings** - to make it easy to meet online. Minimum feature set: shared screen, shared white board, text chat, video of participants. Bonus features: persistent meeting room (your office online), avatars.

**Blogs** - for narrating your work, maintaining your digital reputation, recording accomplishments, documenting expert knowledge, showing people what you're up to so they can help out

**Bookmarks** - to facilitate searching for links to information, discover what sources other people are following, locate experts

**Mobile access** - Half of America's workforce sometimes works away from the office. Smart phones are surpassing PCs for connecting to networks for access and participation. Phones post most Tweets than computers. Google designs its apps for mobile before porting them to PCs.

**Social network** - for online conversation, connecting with people, and all of the above functions.

## Conclusion

Learning used to focus on what was in an individual's head. The individual took the test, got the degree, or earned the certificate. The new learning focuses on what it takes to do the job right. The workplace is an open-book exam. What worker doesn't have a cell phone and an Internet connection? Using personal information pipelines to get help from colleagues and the Internet to access the world's information is encouraged. Besides, it's probably the team that must perform, not a single individual. Thirty years ago, three-quarters of what a worker need to do the job was stored in her head; now it's less than 10%.

CHAPTER 19

# PARTICIPATION

> Methods of managing projects, including learning projects, range from more formal and structured to casual and unstructured. As a facilitator, you'll see your peeragogy community constantly adjust, as it seeks an equilibrium between order and chaos, ideally allowing everyone to be involved at their own pace without losing focus, and in such a manner that the collective can deliver.

For teachers reading this, and wondering how to use peeragogy to improve participation in their classrooms, it's really quite simple: reframe the educational vision using peeragogical eyes. Recast the classroom as a community of people who learn together, the teacher as facilitator, and the curriculum as a starting point that can be used to organize and trigger community engagement. However, just because it's simple doesn't mean it's easy! Whatever your day job may be, consider: how well do the various groups you participate in work together – even when the members ostensibly share a common purpose? Sometimes things tick along nicely, and, presumably, sometimes it's excruciating. What's your role in all of this? How do *you* participate?

## Guidelines for participation

- Accept that some people want to watch what is going on before jumping in. This doesn't mean you have to keep them hanging around forever. After a while, you may unenroll people who don't add any value to the community. In our Peeragogy project, we've asked people to explicitly re-enroll several times. Most do renew; some leave.

- Accept that people may only contribute a little: if this contribution is good it will add value to the whole.
- Understand that you can not impose strict deadlines on volunteers; adjust targets accordingly.
- Let your work be "open" in the sense described in Wikipedia's Neutral Point of View policy.
- Give roles to participants and define some "energy centers" who will take the lead on specific items in the project.
- Organize regular face-to-face or online meetings to talk about progress and what's needed in upcoming days/weeks.
- Ask participants to be clear about when they will be ready to deliver their contributions.
- Have clear deadlines, but allow contributions that come in after the deadline – in general, be flexible.
- Add a newcomer section on your online platform to help new arrivals get started. Seasoned participants are often eager to serve as mentors.

When we think about project management in an organization, we often relate to well-established tools and processes. For example, we can use the Project Management Body of Knowledge (PMBOK) as a standard. For the Project Management Institute (PMI) and many workers, these standards are seen as the key to project success. In classical project management, tasks and deadlines are clearly defined. We will, for example, use Program Evaluation and Review Technic (PERT) to analyze and represent tasks. We often represent the project schedule using a Gantt chart. Those are just two of the project management tools that illustrate how "mainstream" project management rests firmly on an engineering background. In these very structured projects, each actor is expected to work exactly as planned and to deliver his part of the work on time; every individual delay can potentially lead to a collective delay.

Peeragogy projects may be, naturally, a bit different from other settings, although we can potentially reuse both formal and informal methods of organization. For example, unlike a typical wiki – or classroom – peeragogy projects often expect to break the 90/9/1 rule. Keep in mind that some participants may not contribute all the time – but one really good idea can be a major contribution. See the anti-pattern "Misunderstanding Power" for some further reflections on these matters.

How are we doing? If we take our Google+ Community have contributed to the handbook as the basic population, then as of January 2014, over 4% have contributed – pretty good. However, we have yet to reach a contribution profile like 70/20/10. It's important to remember that – especially in a volunteer organization – no one can "make"' other people participate, and that all the lists of things to do are for nought if no one steps in to do the work. For this reason, if anything is going to happen, what's needed are *realistic* estimates of available work effort. Finally, in closing this section, we want to emphasize that measures of participation offer only a very rough proxy for measures of learning, although the two are clearly related.

CHAPTER 20

# NEW DESIGNS FOR CO-WORKING AND CO-LEARNING

Joseph Corneli

Interpersonal exchange and collaboration to develop and pursue common goals goes further than "learning" or "working" in their mainstream definitions. This article will look at examples drawn from Linux, Wikipedia, and my own work on PlanetMath, with a few surprises along the way, leading us to new ways of thinking about how to do co-design when build systems for peer learning and peer production.

## Co-working as the flip side of convening

**Linus Torvalds**: The first mistake is thinking that you can throw things out there and ask people to help. That's not how it works. You make it public, and then you assume that you'll have to do all the work, and ask people to come up with suggestions of what you should do, not what they should do. Maybe they'll start helping eventually, but you should start off with the assumption that you're going to be the one maintaining it and ready to do all the work. The other thing–and it's kind of related–that people seem to get wrong is to think that the code they write is what matters. No, even if you wrote 100% of the code, and even if you are the best programmer in the world and will never need any help with the project at all, the thing that really matters is the users of the code.

> The code itself is unimportant; the project is only as useful as people actually find it.

In fact, we can think of contributors as a special class of "user" with a real time investment in the way the project works. We typically cannot "Tom Sawyer" ourselves into leisure or ease just because we manage to work collaboratively, or just because we have found people with some common interests. And yet, in the right setting, many people do want to contribute! For example, on "Wikipedia, the encyclopedia anyone can edit" (as of 2011) as many as 80,000 visitors make 5 or more edits per month. This is interesting to compare with the empirical fact that (as of 2006) "over 50% of all the edits are done by just .7% of the users... *24 people*... and in fact the most active 2%, which is 1400 people, have done 73.4% of all the edits." Similar numbers apply to other peer production communities.

## A little theory

In many natural systems, things are not distributed equally, and it is not atypical for e.g. 20% of the population to control 80% of the wealth (or, as we saw, for 2% of the users to do nearly 80% of the edits). Many, many systems work like this, so maybe there's a good reason for it. Let's think about it in terms of "coordination" as understood by the late Elinor Ostrom. She talked about "local solutions for local problems". By definition, such geographically-based coordination requires close proximity. What does "close" mean? If we think about homogeneous space, it just means that we draw a circle (or sphere) around where we are, and the radius of this circle (resp. sphere) is small.

An interesting mathematical fact is that as the dimension grows, the volume of the sphere gets "thinner", so the radius must increase to capture the same $d$-dimensional volume when $d$ grows! In other words, the more different factors impact on a given issue, the less likely there are to be small scale, self-contained, "local problems" or "local solutions" in the first place.

As a network or service provider grows (like a MOOC as opposed to a Collaborative Exploration, for example), they typically build many weak ties, with a few strong ties that hold it all together. Google is happy to serve everyone's web requests – but they can't have just anyone walking in off the street and connecting devices their network in Mountain View.

By the way, the 2006 article about Wikipedia quoted above was written by Aaron Swartz ("over 50% of all the edits are done by... 24 people", etc.), who achieved considerable notoriety for downloading lots and lots of academic papers with a device plugged into MIT's network. His suicide while under federal prosecution for this activity caused considerable shock, grief, and dismay among online activists. One thing we could potentially take away from the experience is that there is a tremendous difference between a solo effort and the distributed peer-to-peer infrastructures like the ones that underly the PirateBay, which, despite raids, fines, jail sentences, nation-wide bans, and server downtime, has proved decidedly hard to extinguish. According to a recent press release: "If they cut off one head, two more shall take its place."

## Co-working: what is an institution?

As idealists, we would love to be able to create systems that are both powerful and humane. Some may reflect with a type of sentimental fondness on completely mythical economic systems in which a "dedicated individual could rise to the top through dint of effort." But well-articulated systems like this *do* exist: natural languages, for example, are so expressive and adaptive that most sentences have never been said before. A well-articulated system lends itself to "local solutions to local problems" – but in the linguistics case, this is only because all words are not created equal.

> **Dr Seuss**: My brothers read a little bit. Little words like 'If' and 'It.' My father can read big words, too, Like CONSTANTINOPLE and TIMBUKTU.

We could go on here to talk about Coase's theory of the firm, and Benkler's theory of "Coase's Penguin". We might continue quoting from Aaron Swartz. But we will not get so deeply into that here: you can explore it on your own! For now, it is enough to say that an institution is a bit like a language. This will help us a lot in the next section.

## Designing a platform for peer learning

> PlanetMath *is a virtual community which aims to help make mathematical knowledge more accessible.*

In my PhD thesis [1], I talk about my work to turn this long-running website, which since 2001 had focused on building a mathematics encyclopedia, into a peer produced peer learning environment. We wanted to retain all of the old activities related to authoring, reviewing, and discussing encyclopedia articles, but we would also add a bunch of new features having to do with mathmatical problem solving, an activity that is suitable for mathematical beginners.

My first translation of this idea into a basic interaction design was as follows. People can continue to add articles to PlanetMath's encyclopedia: they can connect one article to another (A→A) either by making one article the "parent" of another, or, more typically, via an inline link. Like in the old system, users can discuss any object (X→T), but now there is more structure: *problems* can be connected to articles (A→P) and *solutions* can be connected to problems (P→S). Instead of explicitly modeling "goals," I decided that problems and articles could be organized into "collections," the same way that videos are organized into playlists on YouTube, and that the user would get encouraging directed feedback as they work their way through the problems in a given collection. I described a few other types of objects and interactions, like questions and answers, groups, and the ability to change the "type" of certain contributed objects.

The next step was to do a complete overhaul of PlanetMath's software system, to build something that could actually *do* all of that. After deploying the realized system and doing some studies with PlanetMath users, I realized the design summarized above was not complete. Note that this is very much along the lines of what Linus Torvalds said above: I did the design, and me and a small group of collaborators with their own vested interests built the system, then we put it out there to get more ideas from users.

The main thing that was missing from the earlier design was the idea of a *project*. From interviewing users, it became clear to me that it would be helpful to think of every object as being part of at least one project: everything should have someone looking after it! Importantly, getting back to the very beginning of this article, each project can define its own purpose for existing. Here's how I put it in my thesis:

> *Actions and artifacts are embedded within projects, which can be modeled in terms of informal user experience and formal system features. Project updates can be modeled with a language of fundamental actions. Projects themselves model their outcomes, and are made "viable" by features that connect to the motivations and ambitions of potential participants.*

The key point is that the evolving design describes a sort "grammar" for the kinds of things that can be done on PlanetMath. In the updated design, projects are something like paragraphs that combine simple sentences. The language can be extended further, and I hope that will happen in further study. In particular, we need to understand more about how the "sublanguage" of project updates works (compare the Roadmap pattern described in this handbook).

## The discussion continues: Reliving the history of mathematics as a peeragogical game?

These notes have shown one approach to the design of spaces for learning and knowledge building. Although the article has focused on mathematics learning, similar reflections would apply to designing other sorts of spaces for learning or working, for instance, to the continued development of the Peeragogy project itself! Perhaps it can contribute to the development of a new kind of institution.

> **Doug Breitbart**: It occurred to me that you could add a learning dimension to the site that sets up the history of math as a series of problems, proofs and theorems that, although already solved, could be re-cast as if not yet solved, and framed as current challenges which visitors could take on (clearly with links to the actual solutions, and deconstruction of how they were arrived at, when the visitor decides to throw in the towel).

## References

1. Corneli, J. (2014). Peer Produced Peer Learning: A Mathematics Case Study. Ph. D. thesis. The Open University.

CHAPTER 21

# A CO-WORKING STORY

JULIAN ELVE

The board of a housing association needs to set a strategy that takes account of major changes in legislation, the UK benefits system and the availability of long term construction loans. Julian, eager to make use of his new-found peeragogical insights suggests an approach where individuals research specific factors and the team work together to draw out themes and strategic options. As a start he proposes that each board member researches an area of specific knowledge or interest.

Jim, the Chairman, identifies questions he wants to ask the Chairs of other Housing Associations. Pamela (a lawyer) agrees to do an analysis of the relevant legislation. Clare, the CEO, plans out a series of meetings with the local councils in the boroughs of interest to understand their reactions to the changes from central government. Jenny, the operations director, starts modelling the impact on occupancy from new benefits rules. Colin, the development director, re-purposes existing work on options for development sites to reflect different housing mixes on each site. Malcolm, the finance director, prepares a briefing on the new treasury landscape and the changing positions of major lenders.

Each member of the board documents their research in a private wiki. Julian facilitates some synchronous and asynchronous discussion to draw out themes in each area and map across the areas of interest. Malcolm, the FD, adapts his financial models to take different options as parameters. Clare refines the themes into a set of strategic options for the association, with associated financial modelling provided by Malcolm. Individual board members explore the options asynchronously before convening for an all-day meeting to confirm the strategy.

# Part VII

# Assessment

CHAPTER 22

# INTRODUCTION TO PEERAGOGICAL ASSESSMENT

This article is about both assessment in peer learning and an exercise in assessment, as we put our strategy for assessment into practice by evaluating the Peeragogy Handbook itself.

## Adapting strategies for learning assessment to the peer-learning context

In "Effective Grading: A Tool for Learning and Assessment," Barbara E. Walvoord and Virginia Johnson Anderson have outlined an approach to grading. They address three questions:

1. Who needs to know, and why?
2. Which data are collected?
3. How does the assessment body analyze data and present findings?

The authors suggest that institutions, departments, and assessment committees should begin with these simple questions and work from them towards anything more complex. These simple questions provide a way to understand - and assess - any strategy for assessment! For example, consider "formative assessment" (in other words, keeping track of how things are going). In this context, the answers to the questions above would be:

1. Teachers need to know about the way students are thinking about their work, so they can deliver better teaching.
2. Teachers gather a lot of these details on learning activities by "listening over the shoulders" of students.

3. Teachers apply analysis techniques that come from their training or experience – and they do not necessarily present their assessments to students directly, but rather, feed it back in the form of improved teaching.

This is very much a "teacher knows best" model! In order to do something like formative assessment among peers, we would have to make quite a few adjustments.

1. At least some of the project participants would have to know how other participants are thinking about their work as well as analyzing their own progress. We are then able to "deliver better teaching" and work together to problem-solve when difficulties arise.
2. It may be most convenient for each participant to take on a share of the work (e.g. by maintaining a "learning journal" which might be shared with other participants). This imposes a certain overhead, but as we remarked elsewhere, "meta-learning is a font of knowledge!" Outside of persistent self-reflection, details about others' learning can sometimes be abstracted from their contributions to the project ("learning analytics" is a whole topic unto itself).
3. If a participant in a "learning project" is bored, frustrated, feeling closed-minded, or for whatever other reason "not learning," then there is definitely a question. But for whom? For the person who isn't learning? For the collective as a whole? We may not have to ponder this conundrum for long: if we go back to the idea that "learning is adaptation," someone who is not learning in a given context will likely leave and find another context where they can learn more.

This is but one example of an assessment strategy: in addition to "formative assessment", "diagnostic" and "summative" strategies are also quite popular in mainstream education. The main purpose of this section has been to show that when the familiar roles from formal education devolve "to the people," the way assessment looks can change a lot. In the following section, we offer and begin to implement an assessment strategy for evaluating the peeragogy project as a whole.

## Case study in peeragogical evaluation: the Peeragogy project itself

We can evaluate this project partly in terms of its main "deliverable," the Peeragogy Handbook (which you are now reading). In particular, we can ask: Is this handbook useful for its intended audience? If so, in what ways? If not, how can we adapt? The "intended audience" could potentially include anyone who is participating in a peer learning project, or who is thinking about starting one. We can also evaluate the learning experience that the co-creators of this handbook have had. Has working on this book been a useful experience for those involved? These are two very different questions, with two different targets for analysis – though the book's co-creators are also part of the "intended audience". Indeed, we might start by asking "how has working on this book been useful for us?"

### A methodological interlude: "Follow the money"

The metrics for learning in corporations are business metrics based on financial data. Managers want to know: Has the learning experience enhanced the workers' productivity? When people ask about the ROI of informal learning, ask them how they measure the ROI of formal learning. Test scores, grades, self-evaluations, attendance, and certifications prove nothing. The ROI of any form of learning is the value of changes in behavior divided by the cost of inducing the change. Like the tree falling over in the forest with no one to hear it, if there's no change in behavior over the long haul, no learning took place. ROI is in the mind of the beholder, in this case, the sponsor of the learning who is going to decide whether or not to continue investing. Because the figure involves judgment, it's never going to be accurate to the first decimal place. Fortunately, it doesn't have to be. Ballpark numbers are solid enough for making decisions.

The process begins before the investment is made. What degree of change will the sponsor accept as worthy of reinvestment? How are we going to measure that? What's an adequate level of change? What's so low we'll have to adopt a different approach? How much of the change can we attribute to learning? You need to gain agreement on these things beforehand. Monday morning quarterbacking is not credible. It's counterproductive to assess learning immediately after it occurs. You can see if people are engaged or if they're complaining about getting lost, but you cannot assess what sticks until the forgetting curve has ravaged the learners' memories for a few months. Interest also doesn't guarantee results in learning, though it helps. Without reinforcement, people forget most of what they learn in short order. It's beguiling to try to correlate the impact of learning with existing financial metrics like increased revenues or better customer service scores. Done on its own, this approach rarely works because learning is but one of many factors that influence results, even in the business world. Was today's success due to learning or the ad campaign or weak competition or the sales contest or something else? The best way to assess how people learn is to ask them. How did you figure out how to do this? Who did you learn this from? How did that change your behavior? How can we make it better? How will you? Self-evaluation through reflective practice can build both metacognition and self-efficacy in individuals and groups. Too time consuming? Not if you interview a representative sample. For example, interviewing less than 100 people out of 2000 yields an answer within 10% nineteen times out of twenty, a higher confidence level than most estimates in business. Interviewing 150 people will give you the right estimate 99% of the time.

## Roadmaps in Peer Learning

We have identified several basic and more elaborated patterns that describe "the Peeragogy effect". These have shaped the way we think about things since. We think the central pattern is the Roadmap, which can apply at the individual level, as a personal learning plan, or at a project level. As we've indicated, sometimes people simply plan to see what happens: alternative versions of the Roadmap might be a compass, or even the ocean chart from the *Hunting of the Snark*. The roadmap may just be a North Star, or it may include detailed reasons "why," further exposition about the goal, indicators of progress, a section for future work, and so forth. Our initial roadmap for the project was the preliminaly outline of the handbook; as the handbook approached completion at the "2.0" level, we spun off additional goals into a new roadmap for a Peeragogy Accelerator. Additional patterns flesh out the project's properties in an open "agora" of possibilities. Unlike the ocean, our map retains traces of where we've been, and what we've learned. In an effort to document these "paths in the grass," we prepared a short survey for Peeragogy project participants.

We asked people how they had participated (e.g., by signing up for access to the Social Media Classroom and mailing list, joining the Google+ Community, authoring articles, etc.) and what goals or interests motivated their participation. We asked them to describe the Peeragogy project itself in terms of its aims and to evaluate its progress over the first year of its existence. As another measure of "investment" in the project, we asked, with no strings attached, whether the respondent would consider donating to the Peeragogy project. This survey was circulated to 223 members of the Peeragogy Google+ community, as well as to the currently active members of the Peeragogy mailing list. The responses outlining the project's purpose ranged from the general: "How to make sense of learning in our complex times?" – to much more specific:

> **Anonymous Survey Respondent 1**: Push education further, providing a toolbox and techniques to self-learners. In the peeragogy.org introduction page we assume that self-learners are self-motivated, that may be right but the Handbook can also help them to stay motivated, to motivate others and to face obstacles that may erode motivation.

Considering motivation as a key factor, it is interesting to observe how various understandings of the project's aims and its flaws intersected with personal motivations. For example, one respondent (who had only participated by joining the Google+ community) was: "[Seeking] [i]nformation on how to create and engage communities of interest with a shared aim of learning." More active participants justified their participation in terms of what they get out of taking an active role, for instance:

> **Anonymous Survey Respondent 2**: "Contributing to the project allows me to co-learn, share and co-write ideas with a colourful mix of great minds. Those ideas can be related to many fields, from communication, to technology, to psychology, to sociology, and more."

The most active participants justified their participation in terms of beliefs or a sense of mission:

> **Anonymous Survey Respondent 3**: "Currently we are witnessing many efforts to incorporate technology as an important tool for the learning process. However, most of the initiatives are reduced to the technical aspect (apps, tools, social networks) without any theoretical or epistemological framework. Peeragogy is rooted in many theories of cooperation and leads to a deeper level of understanding about the role of technology in the learning process. I am convinced of the social nature of learning, so I participate in the project to learn and find new strategies to learn better with my students."

Or again:

> **Anonymous Survey Respondent 4**: "I wanted to understand how peer production really works. Could we create a well-articulated system that helps people interested in peer production get their own goals accomplished, and that itself grows and learns? Peer

production seems linked to learning and sharing - so I wanted to understand how that works."

They also expressed criticism of the project, implying that they may feel rather powerless to make the changes that would correct course:

> **Anonymous Survey Respondent 5**: "Sometimes I wonder whether the project is not too much 'by education specialists for education specialists.' I have the feeling peer learning is happening anyway, and that teens are often amazingly good at it. Do they need 'learning experts' or 'books by learning experts' at all? Maybe they are the experts. Or at least, quite a few of them are."

Another respondent was more blunt:

> **Anonymous Survey Respondent 6**: "What problems do you feel we are aiming to solve in the Peeragogy project? We seem to not be sure. How much progress did we make in the first year? Some... got stuck in theory."

But, again, it is not entirely clear how the project provides clear pathways for contributors to turn their frustrations into changed behavior or results. Additionally we need to be entirely clear that we are indeed paving new ground with our work. If there are proven peer learning methods out there we have not examined and included in our efforts, we need to find and address them. Peeragogy is not about reinventing the wheel. It is also not entirely clear whether excited new peers will find pathways to turn their excitement into shared products or process. For example, one respondent (who had only joined the Google+ community) had not yet introduced current, fascinating projects publicly:

> **Anonymous Survey Respondent 7**: "I joined the Google+ community because I am interested in developing peer to peer environments for my students to learn in. We are moving towards a community-based, place-based program where we partner with community orgs like our history museum for microhistory work, our local watershed community and farmer's markets for local environmental and food issues, etc. I would love for those local efforts working with adult mentors to combine with a peer network of other HS students in some kind of cMOOC or social media network."

Responses such as this highlight our need to make ourselves available to hear about exciting new projects from interested peers, simultaneously giving them easier avenues to share. Our work on developing a peeragogy accelerator in the next section is an attempt to address this situation.

### Summary

We can reflect back on how this feedback bears on the main sections of this book with a few more selected quotes. These motivate further refinement to our strategies for working on this project, and help build a constructively-critical jumping off point for future projects that put peeragogy into action.

**Cooperate** *How can we build strong collaboration?*

> "A team is not a group of people who work together. A team is not a group of people who work together. A team is a group of people who trust each other."

**Convene** *How can we build a more practical focus?*

> "The insight that the project will thrive if people are working hard on their individual problems and shar-

ing feedback on the process seems like the key thing going forward. This feels valuable and important."

**Organize** *How to connect with newcomers and oldcomers?*

> "I just came on board a month ago. I am designing a self-organizing learning environment (SOLE) or PLE/PLN that I hope will help enable communities of life long learners to practice digital literacies."

**Assess** *How can we be effective and relevant?*

> "I am game to also explore ways to attach peeragogy to spaces where funding can flow based on real need in communities."

## Conclusion

We can estimate individual learning by examining the real problems solved by the individual. It makes sense to assess the way groups solve problems in a similar way. Solving real problems often happens very slowly, with lots of practice along the way. We've learned a lot about peer learning in this project, and the assessment above gives a serious look at what we've accomplished, and at how much is left.

CHAPTER 23

# RESEARCHING PEERAGOGY

Joseph Corneli

This is an unfinished essay from 2001, found nearly a decade and a half later in a box of odds and ends. The essay foreshadows our ongoing research on peer produced peer learning, and also helps to highlight some of the difficulties associated with this enterprise.

## RESEARCH SKILL DEVELOPMENT PROGRAM

**THE POINT.** This is an effort at understanding how research skills in the mathematical sciences [but it could be any topic] can be acquired by students.

**WHO WE ARE.** We are students at a state-funded liberal arts college based in Sarasota, Florida. Our school is called New College. The emphasis of the program at New College is self-directed learning.

**SELF-DIRECTED LEARNING.** Since people have free will and learn from experience, self-directed learning could be said to take place wherever people engage in any activity. However, this view is unfounded, and the implication is false. Unstructured learning is more accurately undirected. If learning is structured, say by a teacher, this does not imply that it is self-directed, even given the free will of the learner to participate. The choice to participate in learning is not the same as directing the learning. Structure can impose the direction on a (passive) learner. This does not mean that the presence of a teacher or a system to learn implies that the student's learning is not self-directed.

The criterion we are looking for is that the student have an active, ongoing and purposive role in deciding the structure of his/her/its [e.g. in the case of computer programs] learning environment. A teacher must be informed by and responsive to the student's feedback, or the learning the student does under that teacher's instruction is not self-directed.

**INTEGRATION OF RESEARCH AND EDUCATION.** In deciding upon a course of study, it behooves the student, as he/she/it examines a potential activity, to consider questions such as these, with the utmost care:

- What is the intellectual merit of the proposed activity?
- Is there sufficient access to resources?
- How well-conceived and organized is the proposed activity?
- To what extent does the proposed activity suggest and explore creative and original concepts?
- To what extent will it enhance possibilities for future work?
- What are the broader impacts of the proposed activity?
- What is the product?

If these questions are addressed well, the student will enter upon a focused program and will have already at the beginning devised a coherent plan for its satisfactory completion. Furthermore, the product is likely to be a net benefit to society. The idea of traditional education is that it is the student, with an increased knowledge and skill base, who constitutes the product. His/her/its knowledge and skills (upon exiting the educational program) are valued by society, and he/she/it is willing to put forth during the program a commensurate amount of blood, sweat, and tears (not to mention tuition and time) to extract the valuable knowledge and skills. In scientific fields, one of these skills is supposed to be the ability to do research. The idea that "the best proof of someone's research ability is the research they have done" has played a significant role in the way scientific education, and the scientific enterprise, has been run in recent years. Research experience at the undergraduate level is one of the top criteria considered by graduate programs in science when they decide which candidates to admit. It is not without reason, then, that national programs for undergraduate researchers (most notably, the National Science Foundation's Research Experiences for Undergraduates (REU) summer programs) are highly competitive, taking only the best qualified applicants nationwide. Many technical and land-grant universities have internally- or industry-funded Undergraduate Research Opportunities Programs (UROP) which offer financial awards to undergraduate students, which enable them to collaborate with faculty on specialized research projects in their joint field of interest, or to do original work on their won. These programs make it possible for students to make research a part of their background. In particular, such programs give students a chance to see what it is like to work on open problems (usually the problems devised by the program administrator or principal investigator; occasionally on questions proposed by the student researchers themselves). It goes without saying that such experiences are typically only part of the curriculum. The NSF's vision of integrating research and education is to have individuals concurrently assume responsibilities as researchers, educators, and students, where all engage in joint efforts that infuse education with the excitement of discovery and enrich research through the diversity of learning perspectives. The benefits of such a system are manifold. It is however very difficult to implement in most educational contexts. A place like New College, where the culture already is disposed towards student self-direction, may be unique in its ability to foster an undergraduate scientific curriculum based primarily on research. The questions listed at the beginning of this section are the questions a research must answer when initiating a research program for undergraduates. (They were lifted from the NSF's summary of how they review

REU proposals.) By pointing out here that the same questions are the natural questions for a student to ask when considering how to invest his/her/its time and energy, we mean to point to the unique possibility afforded the self-directed learner, namely: he/she/it can act as a researcher, an educator, and a student concurrently, and, to a degree that is possible for very few, harmoniously.

**RESEARCH AS A WAY OF LIFE (ADDITIONAL REVIEW CRITERIA SPECIFIC TO REU).** There are other criteria considered by the NSF, for example, the qualifications of the person who proposes the research project. This is *prima facie* difficult for undergraduates to fulfil satisfactorily. Further criteria include:

- The appropriateness and value of the educational experience for the student participants, particularly the appropriateness of the research project(s) for undergraduate involvement and the nature of student participation in these activities.

- The quality of the research environment, including the record of the mentor(s) with undergraduate research participation, the facilities, and the professional development opportunities.

- Appropriateness of the student recruitment and selection plan, including plans for involving students from underrepresented groups and from institutions with limited research opportunities.

- Quality of plans for student preparation and follow-through designed to promote continuation of student interest and involvement in research.

- For REU sites, effectiveness of institutional commitment and of plans for managing the project and evaluating outcomes.

## Some afterthoughts, with the benefit of hindsight (2015)

The idea that an undergraduate student could run an REU program is perhaps not entirely ridiculous, but it is still extremely unlikely to work – as the essay points out. What is possible is for a student or group of students to set up a website and collaborate informally online. This is what Aaron Krowne did in around 2001, with PlanetMath.org. I joined a few years later, as a graduate student in mathematics. PlanetMath was a little bit like an always-on version of the project outlined in the essay above. The main emphasis was on building a mathematics encyclopedia, but some contributors were doing original research and collaborating with each other. The site administrators and assorted devotees were also doing a lot of meta-level thinking about how the project could improve. In 2005 or thereabouts, I started a wiki called AsteroidMeta to help organize those discussions. By this time, I was no longer in the mathematics graduate programme: I had more or less stopped going to classes a year earlier. My interests had more to do with how computers could change the way people do mathematics than in doing mathematics the way it had always been done. Myself and a few other PlanetMath contributors published research papers on this theme in a symposium on Free Culture and the Digital Library that Aaron helped organize at Emory, where he was then Head of Digital Library Research. Working on informal collaborations like this, and doing related open source software development, I built a CV that helped me get into another postgrad program in 2010. This time, in the United Kingdom, where I was able to largely set my own research agenda from the start. I focused on rebuilding the PlanetMath website (as described in the *Handbook* chapter on "New Designs for Co-Working and Co-Learning"). Presenting some of this work at Wikimania 2010, I met Charlie Danoff, and when we later met online at P2PU, we decided to sit in on each others first round of courses. As the term progressed, we collaboratively developed a critique of the way things worked at P2PU and suggested some principles that would guide improvement. We called this "paragogy." When Howard Rheingold learned about this work from

Charlie, who was taking one of his online classes at RheingoldU, he suggested the more accessible name "peeragogy." To our pleasant surprise Howard then drew on his network of friends and fans to kick off the Peeragogy project. Naturally, I joined, and was able to draw on what we learned in my thesis. Unlike the previous time around, I also had a lot of formal support from my supervisors, as well as a lot of self-organized support from others, and I completed the program successfully. In doing so, I began to accrue the credentials that would be necessary for organizing a formally-funded research project like the one outlined in the essay above. Doing this in the undergraduate research setting would, of course, require interested undergraduates. At the moment, I'm employed as a computer science researcher, exploring the development of peer learning and peer production with the computational "its" mentioned in the essay. The Peeragogy project continues to be a great resource for collaborative research on research and collaboration.

# Part VIII

# Technologies, Services, and Platforms

CHAPTER 24

# INTRODUCTION TO TECHNOLOGIES FOR PEERAGOGY

GIGI JOHNSON

**It is tempting to bring a list of technologies out as a glorious cookbook.** We need a 1/2 cup of group writing tools, 2 tsp. of social network elements, a thick slice of social bookmarking, and some sugar, then put it in the oven for 1 hour for 350 degrees.

We have created a broad features/functions list for Handbook readers to reflect upon and consider. The joy of this list is that you can consider alternatives for the way you communicate and work while you are planning the project, or can add in new elements to solve communications gaps or create new tools.

However, too many tools spoil the broth. In the writing of this Handbook, we found that out firsthand. We spent a lot of marvelous energy exploring different tools to collaborate, curate information, do research, tag resources, and adjudicate among all of our points of view. In looking at groups working with the various MOOCs, as another example, different groups of students often camp in different social media technologies to work.

In large courses, students often have to be pushed into various social media tools to "co-create" with great protest and lots of inertia. And finally, co-learning groups often come from very different backgrounds, ages, and stages of life, with very different tools embedded in their current lives. Do we have time for three more tools in our busy days? Do more tools help – or do they interfere with our work?

In this section, we'll share with you a few issues:

- What technologies are most useful in peer learning? What do we use them for? What features or functions help our co-learning process?

- How do we decide (a) as a group and (b) for the group on what tools we can use? Do we decide upfront, or grow as we go?
- How do we coach and scaffold each other on use of tools?
- How much do the tool choices impact the actual outcome of our learning project?
- What are the different roles that co-learners can take in co-teaching and co-coaching the technology affordances/assumptions in the project to make others' lives easier?

Keep in mind – your needs for tools, plus how the way the group uses them, will change as the co-learning project moves along. Technologies themselves tend to change rapidly. Are you willing to change tools during the project as your needs and users change, or do you plan to use a given tool set from the beginning to the end of your project?

## Features and Considerations

We will begin below with a discussions of "features" and initial considerations, and then move to a broader "Choose Your Own Adventure"-style matrix of features leading to a wide variety of collaboration-based technology tools online.

### Technologies and Features

As we will share in the extensive list below, there are abundant tools now available – both for free and for pay – to bring great features to our co-learning endeavors. It is tempting to grab a group of fancy tools and bring the group into a fairly complex tool environment to find the perfect combination of resources. The challenge: adult learners seek both comfort and context in our lives [1], [2]. In choosing tool "brands", we can ignore the features themselves and what we need as parts of the puzzle for learning. We also can have anxiety about our self-beliefs around computers and technology, which in turn can limit our abilities [3].

Before we get to brands and choices, it helps to ask a few questions about the learning goals and environments:

- What do we need as features, and at what stage of the learning process?
- What are we already comfortable with, individually and as a group?
- Do we want to stay with comfortable existing tools, or do we want to stretch, or both?
- What types of learners do we have in this group? Technologically advanced? Comfortable with basics?
- Do we want to invest the time to bring the whole group up to speed on tools? Do all the group members agree on this? Do we want to risk alienating members by making them invest time in new resources?
- We know that our use will migrate and adapt. Do we want to plan for adaptation? Observe it? Learn from it? Make that change intentional as we go?

Researchers over the years have heavily examined these questions of human, technology, and task fit in many arenas. Human-Computer Interaction researchers have looked at "fit" and "adaptive behavior," as well as how the tools can affect how the problem is presented by Te'eni [4]. Creativity support tools [5] have a whole line of design research, as has the field of Computer-Supported Collaborative Work Systems (CSCW). For co-learners and designers interested in the abundance in this space, we've added some additional links below. We here will make this a bit easier. For your co-learning environment, you may want to do one or two exercises in your decision planning:

What *features do you need*? Do you need collaboration? Graphic models? Places to work at the same time (synchronous)? Between meetings (asynchronous)? What are the group members *already using* as their personal learning platforms? It also makes sense to do an inventory about what the group already has as their learning platforms. I'm doing that with another learning group right now. People are much more comfortable – as we also have found in our co-creation of this Handbook – creating and co-learning in tools with which they already are comfortable. Members can be co-teachers to each other – as we have have – in new platforms. What *type of tools*, based on the features that we need, shall we start out with? Resnick *at al.* [6] looked at tools having:

- Low thresholds (easy to get people started)
- Wide walls (able to bring in lots of different situations and uses) and
- High ceilings (able to do complex tasks as the users and uses adapt and grow).

What are important features needed for co-creation and *working together*? In other pages above, we talk abundantly about roles and co-learning challenges. These issues also are not new; Dourish & Bellottii [7] for example, shared long-standing issues in computer-supportive collaborative work online about how we are aware of the information from others, passive vs. active generation of information about collaborators, etc. These challenges used to be "solved" by software designers in individual tools. Now that tools are open, abundant, and diverse, groups embrace these same challenges when choosing between online resources for co-learning.

### Useful Uses and fancy Features of Technological Tools

From here, we will help you think about what might be possible, linking to features and solution ideas.

We start with ways to ask the key questions: What do you want to do and why? We will start with features organized around several different axes:

1. Time/Place

2. Stages of Activities and Tasks
3. Skill Building/Bloom's Taxonomy
4. Use Cases, and
5. Learning Functions.

Each will link to pages that will prompt you with features, functionality, and technology tool ideas.

## Time/Place

We can further break down tools into whether they create or distribute, or whether we can work simultaneously (synchronous) or at our own times (ascynchronous). To make elements of time and place more visual, Baecker [8] created a CSCW Matrix, bringing together time and place functions and needs. Some tools are synchronous, such as Google+ Hangouts, Blackboard Collaborate, and Adobe Connect, while others let us work asynchronously, such as wikis and forums. Google Docs can work be used both ways. We seem to be considering here mostly tools good for group work, but not for solo, while many others are much easier solo or in smaller groups.

Some tools are synchronous, such as Google+ Hangouts, Blackboard Collaborate, and Adobe Connect, while others let us work asynchronously, such as wikis, forums, and Google Docs. We seem to be considering here mostly tools good for group work, but not for solo, while many others are much easier solo or in smaller groups.

## Stages of Activities and Tasks

Ben Shneiderman [5] has simplified the abundant models in this area (e.g., Couger and Cave) with a clear model of 4 general activities and 8 tasks in creation for individuals, which we can lean on as another framework for co-creation in co-learning.

Tools and functions won't be clear cut between areas. For example, some tools are more focused on being generative, or for creating content. Wikis, Etherpad, Google docs, and others usually have a commenting/talk page element, yet generating content is the primary goal and discursive/consultative functions are in service of that. Some tools are discursive, or focused on working together for the creative element of "relating" above – Blackboard Collaborate, the social media class room forums, etc.

### Skill Building (Cognitive, a la Bloom's Taxonomy, see below)

Given that we are exploring learning, we can look to Bloom's Taxonomy (revised, see [9]) for guidance as to how we can look at knowledge support. Starting at the bottom, we have:

- Remembering, as a base;
- Understanding,
- Applying,
- Analyzing,
- Evaluating, and then, at the top,
- Creating.

We could put "search" in the Remembering category above. Others contest that Search, done well, embraces most of the Bloom's elements above. Samantha Penney has created a Bloom's Digital Taxonomy Pyramid infographic, describing tools for learning, which you may want to check out.

### Use Cases (I want to....)

Technologies can be outlined according to the need they serve or use case they fulfill. Examples: If we need to 'curate', Pearl Trees is an option. To 'publish' or 'create', we can look to a wiki or wordpress. Other choices might be great in order to 'collaborate', etc.

One challenge is that tools are not that simple. As we look more closely at the technologies today, we need to reach more broadly to add multiple tags to them. For example Twitter can be used for "Convening a group," for "micro-blogging," for "research," etc.

- Collaborate with a Group
- Create Community
- Curate Information
- Research
- Publish Information
- Create Learning Activities
- Make Something

These plans get more complex, as you are making a group of decisions about tool functionality in order to choose what combination works for use cases. It may be most useful to use a concept map (a tech tool) to think about the needs and combinations that you would bring together to achieve each Use Case or Learning Module.

### Technology Features/Functions

We have not made this easy! There are lots of moving elements and options here, none of them right for everything, and some of them fabulous for specific functions and needs. Some have the low thresholds but may not be broad in scope. Some are broad for many uses; others are specific task-oriented tools. That is some of the charm and frustration.

Weaving all of the above together, we have brought together a shared taxonomy for us to discuss and think about co-learning technology features and functions, which we present as an appendix below. This connects various technology features within an expanded version of Ben Shneiderman's creativity support tools framework. We've created this linked toolset with multiple tags, hopefully making it easier for you to evaluate which tool suits best the necessities of the group. Please consider this a starting point for your own connected exploration.

## Appendix: Features and Functions

Weaving all of these frameworks together, we have brought together a shared taxonomy for us to discuss and think about co-learning technology features and functions. We have connected various technology features with an expanded version of Ben Shneiderman's creativity support tools framework for the linked resource guide. For convenience and to help keep it up to date, we're publishing this resource on Google Docs. We present an overview below.

### References


1. Schein, E. H. (1997). *Organizational learning as cognitive re-definition: Coercive persuasion revisited.* Cambridge, MA: Society for Organizational Learning.
2. Schein, E. H. (2004). *Organizational culture and leadership.* San Francisco, CA: Jossey-Bass.
3. Compeau, D.R., & Higgins, C.A. (1995, June). Computer Self-Efficacy: Development of a Measure and Initial Test. *MIS Quarterly, 19,* (2), 189-211.
4. Te'eni, D. (2006). Designs that fit: An overview of fit conceptualizations in HCI. In *Human-Computer Interaction and Management Information Systems: Foundations,* edited by P. Zhang and D. Galletta, pp. 205-221, Armonk, NY: M.E. Sharpe.
5. Shneiderman, B. (2002). Creativity support tools. *Commun. ACM* 45, 10 (October 2002), 116-120.
6. Resnick, M, Myers, B, Nakakoji, K, Shneiderman, B, Pausch, R, Selker, T. & Eisenberg, M (2005). Design principles for tools to support creative thinking. *Institute for Software Research.* Paper 816.
7. Dourish, P. & Bellotti, V. (1992). Awareness and coordination in shared workspaces. In *Proceedings of the 1992 ACM*

*conference on Computer-supported cooperative work* (CSCW '92). ACM, New York, NY, USA, 107-114.

8. Baecker, R., Grudin, J., Buxton, W., & Greenberg, & (eds.) (1995): *Readings in Human-Computer Interaction: Toward the Year 2000*. New York, NY: Morgan Kaufmann Publishers
9. Anderson, L. W., & Krathwohl, D. R. (Eds.). (2001). *A taxonomy for learning, teaching and assessing: A revision of Bloom's Taxonomy of educational objectives: Complete edition*. New York, NY: Longman.

CHAPTER 25

# FORUMS

HOWARD RHEINGOLD

Forums are web-based communication media that enable groups of people to conduct organized multimedia discussions about multiple topics over a period of time. Selecting the right kind of platform for forum conversations is important, as is know-how about facilitating ongoing conversations online. Forums can be a powerful co-learning tool for people who may have never met face-to-face and could be located in different time zones, but who share an interest in co-learning. Asynchronous media such as forums (or simple email distribution lists or Google Docs) can be an important part of a co-learning toolkit that also include synchronous media from face-to-face meetups to Google+ Hangouts or webinars via Blackboard Collaborate, Adobe Connect, or the open source webconferencing tool, Big Blue Button).

## What is a forum and why should a group use it?

A forum, also known as a message board, bbs, threaded discussion, or conferencing system, affords asynchronous, many-to-many, multimedia discussions for large groups of people over a period of time. That means that people can read and write their parts of the discussion on their own schedule, that everyone in a group can communicate with everyone else, and that graphics, sounds, and videos can accompany text. The best forums index discussion threads by topic, title, tag, date,and/or author and also keep track of which threads and entries (also known as posts) each logged-in participant has already read, making it possible to click on a "show me all the new posts and threads" link each time a participant logs in. This particular form of conversational medium meets the need for organizing conversations after they reach a certain level of complexity. For example, if twenty people want to discuss five subjects over ten days, and each person makes one comment on each subject every day, that makes for one thousand messages in each participant's mailbox. On email lists, when the conversation drifts from the original topic, the subject line usually does not change, so it makes it difficult to find particular discussions later.

Forums make possible a new kind of group discussion that unfolds over days, weeks, and months, in a variety of media. While blogs are primarily about individual voice, forms can be seen as the voice of a group. The best forum threads are not serial collections of individual essays, but constitute a kind of discourse where the discussion becomes more than the sum of its individual posts. Each participant takes into account what others have said, builds on previous posts, poses and answers questions of others, summarize, distill, and concludes.

This short piece on guidelines for discussion board writingis useful, as is this short piece on shaping a culture of conversation. Lively forums with substantial conversation can glue together the disparate parts of a peeragogy group – the sometimes geographically dispersed participants, texts, synchronous chats, blogs, wikis and other co-learning tools and elements. Forum conversations are an art in themselves and forums for learning communities are a specific genre. Reading the resources linked here – and communicating about them – can help any peeragogy group get its forums off to a good start

### How to start fruitful forum discussions:

In most contexts, starting a forum with a topic thread for introductions tends to foster the sense of community needed for valuable conversations. This short piece on how to host good conversations onlineoffers general advice. In addition to introductions, it is often helpful to start a topic thread about which new topic threads to create – when everybody has the power to start a new thread and not everybody knows how forums work, a confusing duplication of conversations can result, so it can be most useful to make the selection of new topic threads a group exercise. A topic thread to ask questions about how to use the forum can prevent a proliferation of duplicate questions. It helps to begin a forum with a few topic threads that invite participation in the context of the group's shared interest "Who is your favorite photographer" for a group of photographers, for example, or "evolution of human intelligence" for a group interested in evolution and/or human intelligence. Ask questions, invite candidate responses to a challenge, make a provocative statement and ask for reactions.

Whether or not you use a rubric for assessing individual participants' forum posts, this guide to how forum posts are evaluated by one professor can help convey the difference between a good and a poor forum conversation:

*4 Points* -The posting(s) integrates multiple viewpoints and weaves both class readings and other participants' postings into their discussion of the subject.

*3 Points* -The posting(s) builds upon the ideas of another participant or two, and digs deeper into the question(s) posed by the instructor.

*2 Points* -A single posting that does not interact with or incorporate the ideas of other participants' comments.

*1 Point* -A simple "me too" comment that neither expands the conversation nor demonstrates any degree of reflection by the student.

*0 Points* -No comment.

## Selecting a forum platform

- You don't want a forum for discussions among two or three people; you do want a forum for discussions among half a dozen or five thousand people.
- You don't want a forum for exchanges of short duration (an hour, a day or two) among any number of people; you do

want a forum for ongoing conversations that can continue for months.
- You don't want a forum if blogs with comment threads will do – blogs with comments afford group discourse, but is not easily indexed and discourse gets complicated with more than a dozen or so bloggers and commenters.

If you do want to select a platform for forum discourse, you will want to decide whether you have the technical expertise available to install the software on your own server or whether you want to look for a hosted solution. Cost is an issue.

Fortunately, an online forum maven by the name of David Wooley has been keeping an up-to-date list of available software and services for more than a decade:

- Forum Software for the Web
- Forum and Message Board Hosting Services

These 2003 suggestions on how to choose a forum by Howard Rheingold can be helpful. If blogs with comments afford a kind of networked individualistic discourse, and video conferencing emulates face-to-face meeting, forums can be seen as a channel for expression of the group voice. When people react to and build on each other's comments, they can learn to act as a collective intelligence as well as a collection of individuals who are communicating in order to learn.

CHAPTER 26

# WIKI

Régis Barondeau

In the context of P2P-learning, a wiki platform can be a useful and powerful collaboration tool. This section will help you understand what a wiki is and what it is not, why you should use it, how to choose a wiki engine and finally how you could use it in a P2P context. Some examples of P2P-learning projects run on wikis will help you see the potential of the tool.

## What is a wiki?

For Ward Cunningham father of the wiki, "a wiki is a freely expandable collection of interlinked Web 'pages', a hypertext system for storing and modifying information - a database, where each page is easily editable by any user with a forms-capable Web browser client" [1].

According to Wikipedia : "a wiki is a website whose users can add, modify, or delete its content via a web browser using a simplified markup language or a rich-text editor" [2].

You can watch this CommonCraft video wiki in plain english to better understand what a wiki is.

## What differentiates the wiki from other co-editing tools?

The previous definitions show that a wiki is a "website," in other words it is composed of pages that are connected together by hyperlinks.In additiont every authorized person (not all wikis are totally open like Wikipedia) can edit the pages from a web browser, reducing time and space constrains. In case one saves a mistake or for any other reason would like to go back to a previous version, a feature called "history" allows users to see previous versions and to roll back any of them. This version history allows also to compare versions avoiding the cluttered of the "commentaries rainbow" we are used too in popular Word processors. For example if you work on a wiki page, and come back later on, you will be able to catch up by comparing your last version with the lastest version of someone else.

Tools like Google Docs or Etherpad are design to enable co-editing on a single document. This can be seen as a "wiki way" of working on a document as it is web based and includes versioning. But it is not a wiki because a single document is not a website. Those tools offer realtime collaboration which wikis do not and are so far easier to use for beginners as they work in WYSIWYG mode, which many wikis do not support. However, the advanced features wiki markup language make it a more powerful tool. In summary, tools like Googles Docs or Etherpad are a great way to quickly collaborate (synchronously, asynchronously, or a mixture of both) on a single document for free, with a low barrier to entry and no technical support. (Note that Etherpad does have a "wiki-links" plugin that can allow it to be used in a more wiki-like way; Hackpad is another real-time editing tool that prominently features linking – and it claims to be "the best wiki ever".)

Using a real wiki engine is more interesting for bigger projects and allows a huge number of users to collaborate on the same platform. A wiki reduces the coordination complication as e-mails exchanges are no more needed to coordinate a project. On the other hand it can help us deal with complexity ([3], [4]) especially if you put basic simple rules in place like the Wikipedia's neutral point of view to allow every participant to share her or his ideas.

Going back to the continuum we talked about before, some tools like Moodle, SharePoint, WordPress, Drupal or others have build in wiki features. Those features can be good but will typically not be as good for wiki-building purposes as a well-developed special-purpose wiki engine. In other words, those tools main focus is not the wiki, which is only a secondary feature.

When you choose a real wiki engine like Mediawiki, Tiki, Foswiki, etc., the wiki will be your platform, not a feature of it. For example if you start a wiki activity in a Moodle course, this wiki will be only visible to a specific group of students and searchable only to those students. On the other hand if your learning platform is a wiki, the whole platform will be searchable to all members regarding their permissions. We are not saying here that a wiki is better than other tools but if you need a wiki engine to address your needs you may consider going with a strong wiki engine rather than a "micro-wiki" engine embedded in an other tool.

## Why use a wiki?

Those are the main reasons you should consider a wiki for your peer learning projects :

- To reduce coordination complication by having a central and always up to date place to store your content. You will reduce e-mail usage drasticly, and have access to your content from everywhere using any operating system.
- To keep track of the evolution of your project and be able to view or roll back any previous version of a wiki page using the history feature.
- To make links between wiki pages to connect ideas and people but also make links to external URL's. This last possibility is very handy to cite your sources.
- To deal with complexity. As a wiki allows anyone to contribute, if you set some easy rules like Wikipedia's NPOV (Neutral Point of View), you will be able to catch more complexity as you will allow everyone to express his or her opinion. Wikis also integrate a forum or comment feature that will help you solve editing conflicts.
- To deal with work in progress. A wiki is a great tool to capture an on going work.
- To support transparency by letting every members of the community see what others are doing.

- To support a network structure as a wiki is by essence an horizontal tool.

Using a hyperlinks you can...

> **Gérard Ayache**: "...jump by a single click from a network node to the other, from a computer to an other, from one information to the other, from one univers to the other, from one brain to the other." (Translated from [5].)

## How to choose a wiki engine?

You will find more than a hundred different wiki engines.

The first main distinction is between open source ones that are free to download and commercial ones you will have to pay for. You will find powerful engines on both sides open source and commercial. Sometimes the open source ones look less polished at first sight but are backed by a strong community and offer a lot of customization possibilities. The commercial are sold like a package, they are nicely presented but often they offer less customization on the user side and additional feature or custom made tools will cost you an extra fee.

The second distinction that we can make is between wiki farms and self-hosted wikis. The wiki farm is a hosting service you can find for both open source or commercial wikis. The goal of those farms is to simplify the hosting of individual wikis. If you don't want to choose a wiki farm hosting, you will have to host the wiki on your own server. This will give you more latitude and data privacy but will require more technical skills and cost you maintenance fees.

The Wikimatrix web site will help you choose the best wiki for your needs. It allows you to compare the features of more than a hundred wiki engines. Here is the top ten list of the best wiki engines by Ward Cunningham.

## How can a wiki be useful in a peeragogy project?

A wiki is a good tool collaborative projects and a specially suited for work in progress as you can easily track changes using the history, compare those version and if necessary roll back a previous versions. In other words, nothing gets lost.

Here are some ideas about how to use a wiki in a peeragogy project :

- **Use a wiki as your learning platform**. It can also support Massive Open Online Courses (MOOCs). A wiki will help you organize your learning context. You can choose to give access to your wiki only to the project participants or open it to the public like Wikipedia. Using hyperlinking, you will operationalize the theory of connectivism by connecting nodes together. As a learning platform wikis are powerful because you can easily see what others are doing, share with them, get inspired, merge ideas or link to ideas. In other words, it creates emulation between learners. For additional ressources about wiki in education follow this Diigo link.

- **Manage your peeragogy project**. A wiki is an excellent tool for project collaboration. Above all, the wiki can be a central place for peer learners to write or link to content. Even if you use several technologies to run your project as we did to write this handbook, at the end of the day, all the content can be centralized on a wiki using direct writing on wiki pages or hyperlinks. This way members can access the content from anywhere and from any device connected to the internet using any platform or application and they will always see the most recent version while being able to browse through the versions history to understand what has changed since their last visit.

- **Publish your project**. As a wiki is a website you can easily use it to show your work to the world. Regarding web design, don't forget that a wiki can look way better than a Wikipedia page if you customize it

## Examples of peeragogy projects run on wikis

Appropedia is a wiki site for collaborative solutions in sustainability, poverty reduction and international development through the use of sound principles and appropriate technology and the sharing of wisdom and project information. The site is open to stakeholders to find, create and improve scalable and adaptable solutions.

Teahouse is a peeragogy project run on a wiki that gives newcomers a place to learn about Wikipedia culture and get feedback from experienced Wikipedians.

## What are the best practices when using a wiki?

- **Cofacilitation** – help each other learn, help each other administer
- **Self-election** – enable people to choose what they want to work on, at their own pace, in their own way
- **Communication** – use comment threads and talk pages to discuss wiki changes
- **Documenting changes** – most wikis enable editors to write very brief descriptions of their edits
- **Rules** – keep rules at a minimum level to avoid chaos without constraining creativity
- **Fun** – make it fun for people to contribute

## References

1. Leuf, Bo, et Ward, Cunningham. 2001. The Wiki way : quick collaboration on the Web. Boston: Addison-Wesley, xxiii, 435 p. p.14
2. Wiki on Wikipedia

3. Andrus, Calvin D. 2005. Toward a complex adaptative intelligence community - The wiki and the blog. Studies in Intelligence. vol. 49, no 3. Online :
4. Barondeau, Régis. 2010. La gestion de projet croise le wiki. École des Sciences de la Gestion, Université du Québec à Montréal, 180 pp.
5. Ayache, Gérard. 2008. Homo sapiens 2.0 : introduction à une histoire naturelle de l'hyperinformation. Paris: Milo, 284 p. p.179

CHAPTER 27

# REAL-TIME MEETINGS

Howard Rheingold

Web services that enable broadband-connected learners to communicate in real time via audio, video, slides, whiteboards, chat, and screen-sharing enable learning groups to add some of the audio-visual dimensions familiar from synchronous face-to-face communication to otherwise asynchronous platforms such as forums, blogs, and wikis. This article includes resources for finding and evaluating appropriate for-free or for-fee platforms, tips on participative activities for real-time meetings, and suggestions for blending real-time and asynchronous media.

## Real-time meeting media

The *Peeragogy Handbook* was conceived and constructed by a group of people on four continents who had not met and had not known about each other before we began meeting online. The process involves asynchronous media, including forums, wikis, social bookmarking groups, and Wordpress, but it probably would never have cohered into a group capable of collective action if it had not been for the real-time meetings where we were able to see each other's faces, hear each other's voices, use a whiteboard as an anonymous agenda-generator, exchange links in chat, show each other examples through screen-sharing. Together, the asynchronous and real-time media enabled us to begin to see ourselves as an effective group. We used both real-time and asynchronous tools to work out processes for creating, refining, and publishing the Handbook, to divide labor, decide on platforms and processes, to collaboratively compose and edit articles, and to design and add graphical and video elements. In particular, we used the Blackboard Collaborate platform, a web-service that enables up to 50 people at a time to meet in a multimedia, recordable, meeting room for around $500/year. We've experimented with other paid platforms, such as Adobe Connect (about the same price as Collaborate), and when we meet in groups of ten or less, we often use the free and recordable Google+ Hangout service. Smaller groups also use Skype or free telephone conferencing services. Mumble is an open source audio-only tool that is popular with gamers. We're watching the development of Big Blue Button, a free and open-source real-time meeting platform, as it develops the full suite of tools that are currently only available for a fee. Dozens of other free, ad-supported and/or freemium webconferencing systems such as Big Marker and Dim-Dim can be found in lists like Howard Rheingold's and Robin Good's (see links at the end of this chapter). Free phone conferencing services provide another technological "lowest common denominator": some provide a few extras like downloadable recordings.

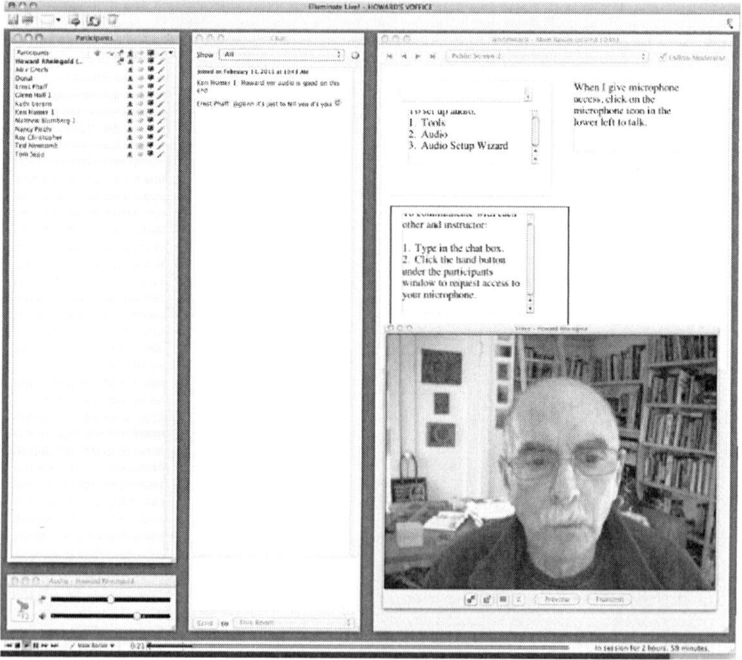

## Features of real-time meeting platforms

There are many free services for chat, screen-sharing, whiteboards, and video conferencing, but combining all these components in separate panes of the same screen (preferably) or as separate tabs of a browser can have a powerful synchronizing and harmonizing effect on the group. The features to look for in meeting platforms include:

**Audio and video**: Choose platforms that enable voice-over-internet-protocol (VOIP) and easy ways for participants to configure their microphones and speakers. Today's webcams, together with adequate lighting and a broadband connection, enable a number of people to be visible at the same time. In Blackboard Collaborate, the person who is speaking at a given moment is visible in the largest video pane, while other participants are available in smaller video windows. Audio and video convey much more of a human dimension than text communications alone. A group of people who have seen and heard each other online are able to work together via asynchronous media such as forums and wikis more effectively. Online face-to-face meetings are often the best way for a group to argue constructively and decide on critical issues. Forums and email are comparatively bad choices for distributed decison-making.

**Slide pushing:** The best platforms will convert .ppt or .pdf files for sequential display. With the addition of text chat, annotations to slides, and the ability to "raise your hand" or interrupt with your voice, an online lecture can be a more multidimensional experience than even a highly discursive in-person lecture.

**Text chat:** As a backchannel, a means of quickly exchanging links to relevant resources, a channel for collaborative note-taking, a way of communicating with the lecturer and with other participants, text chat adds a particularly useful dimension to real-time peeragogical meetings – especially when the division of labor is explicitly agreed upon in advance. We've found that even in meetings that use the real-time collaborative editor Etherpad for collaborative note taking, participants may gravitate toward the built-in chat box for discussion.

**Screen sharing:** The ability of participants to show each other what is on their screens becomes especially important in peer learning, where we all have some things to show each other.

**Web tours:** An alternative to screen-sharing is the ability to display the same web page(s) to all participants by entering URLs.

**Interactive whiteboards**: A shared space that enables participants to enter text, drawings, shapes, colors, to move and resize media, and to import graphic content – especially if it allows anonymous actions – can foster the feeling of participating in a collective intelligence. Collaborative anonymous mind-mapping of the discussion is one technique to try with whiteboards. The whiteboard can also be used to generate an emergent agenda for an "un-meeting".

## Configuring Google+ Hangout - a free alternative for up to 10 people

For up to 10 people, each equipped with a webcam, microphone, and broadband connection, Google+ Hangout can provide high-quality audio-video conferencing. By enabling the text-chat feature and adding Google Docs (text documents, presentations, or spreadsheets), screensharing, and SketchUp (whiteboard), it is possible to emulate most of what the commercial services offer. Adobe Connect and Blackboard Collaborate currently have the user-interface advantage of displaying chat, video, whiteboard/slides as resizable panes on one screen; at present, the free Google services can provide a powerful extension of the basic audio-video platform, but participants have to shift between different tabs or windows in the browser. Note that it is possible to stream a Hangout and record it to YouTube, again at no cost to the user. We've used this tool extensively in the Peeragogy project.

## Suggestions for real-time meetings

In the nine online courses I have facilitated, the emphasis on co-learning encouraged participants to suggest and shape active roles during real-time meetings. By creating and taking on roles, and shifting from role to role, participants engage in a kind of collective learning about collective learning which can be as pleasurable as well as useful. Typically we first brainstorm, then analyze, then organize and present the knowledge that we discover, construct, and ultimately convey together.

## Roles for participants in real-time meetings

- **Searchers:** search the web for references mentioned during the session and other resources relevant to the discussion, and publish the URLs in the text chat
- **Contextualizers:** add two or three sentences of contextual description for each URL
- **Summarizers:** note main points made through text chat.
- **Lexicographers:** identify and collaboratively define words and phrases on a wiki page.
- **Mappers:** keep track of top level and secondary level categories and help the group mindmapping exercise at the end of the session.
- **Curators:** compile the summaries, links to the lexicon and mindmaps, contextualized resources, on a single wiki page.
- **Emergent Agendas:** using the whiteboard for anonymous nomination and preference polling for agenda items, with voice, video, and text-chat channels for discussing nominations, a group can quickly set its own agenda for the real-time session.

## The Paragogical Action Review

Charlie Danoff and Joe Corneli slightly modified the US Army's "After Action Review" into a technique for evaluating peer learning as it happens. The five steps in the "PAR" are:

1. Review what was supposed to happen
2. Establish what is happening
3. Determine what's right and wrong with what we are doing

4. What did we learn or change?
5. What else should we change going forward?

Participants can run through these steps during live meetings to reassess the medium, the readings, the group dynamics, or any other choices that have learning relevance. The focus in the PAR is on change: as such, it provides a simple way to help implement the "double loop learning" described Chris Argris [1].

## Reference

1. Argyris, Chris. "Teaching smart people how to learn." Harvard Business Review, 69.3, 1991.

## Resources

1. `http://delicious.com/hrheingold/webconferencing`
2. `http://www.mindmeister.com/12213323/best-online-collaboration-tools-2012-robin-good-s-collaborative-map`

CHAPTER 28

# CONNECTIVISM IN PRACTICE – HOW TO ORGANIZE A CMOOC

ROLAND LEGRAND

Massive Open Online Courses (MOOCs) are online learning events that can take place synchronously and asynchronously for months. Participants assemble to hear, see, and participate in backchannel communication during live lectures. They read the same texts at the same time, according to a calendar. Learning takes place through self-organized networks of participants, and is almost completely decentralized: individuals and groups create blogs or wikis around their own interpretations of the texts and lectures, and comment on each other's work; each individual and group publicises their RSS feed, which are automatically aggregated by a special (freely available) tool, gRSShopper. Every day, an email goes out to all participants, aggregating activity streams from all the blogs and wikis that engage that week's material. MOOCs are a practical application of a learning theory known as "connectivism" that situates learning in the networks of connections made between individuals and between texts.

Not all MOOCs are Connectivist MOOCs (or *cMOOCs*). Platforms such as Coursera, edX and Udacity offering MOOCs which follow a more traditional, centralized approach (these are sometimes called *xMOOCs*). In this type of MOOC, a professor is taking the lead and the learning-experience is organized top-down. However, some xMOOCs seem to adopt a more blended approach. For instance, the course *E-learning and Digital Cultures* makes use of online spaces beyond the Coursera environment, and the course organizers want some aspects of participation in this course to involve the wider social web.

In this chapter we'll focus on cMOOCs. One might wonder why a course would want to be 'massive' and what '*massive*' means. cMOOC-pioneer Stephen Downes explains that his focus is on the development of a *network structure*, as opposed to a *group structure*, to manage the course. In a network structure there isn't any central focus, for example, a central discussion. That's also the reason why he considers the figure of 150 active participants – *Dunbar's Number* – to be the lower cut-off in order to talk about 'massive':

> **Stephen Downes**: Why Dunbar's number? The reason is that it represents the maximum (theoretical) number of people a person can reasonably interact with. How many blogs can a person read, follow and respond to? Maybe around 150, if Dunbar is correct. Which means that if we have 170 blogs, then the blogs don't constitute a 'core' - people begin to be selective about which blogs they're reading, and different (and interacting) subcommunities can form.

## A learning theory for the digital age

Traditionally, scholars distinguish between three main categories of learning theories: *behaviorism*, *cognitivism* and *constructivism.* Stephen Downes and others would add a fourth one: connectivism, but this is disputed. The central application of connectivism to date is as a theory of what happens in Massive Open Online Courses.

The connectivist theory describes learning as a process of creating connections and developing networks. It is based on the premise that knowledge exists out in the world, rather than inside an individual's mind. Connectivism sees the network as a central metaphor for learning, with a node in the network being a concept (data, feelings, images, etc.) that can be meaningfully related to other nodes. Not all connections are of equal strength in this metaphor; in fact, many connections may be quite weak.

On a practical level, this approach recommends that learning should focus on where to find information (streams), and how to evaluate and mash up those streams, rather than trying to enter lots of (perishable) information into one's skull. Knowing the pipes is more important than knowing what exactly each pipe contains at a given moment. This is the theory. The practice takes place in Connectivist MOOCs (cMOOCs), like Change11. Here, people are free to participate at will. Each week a subject is discussed during synchronous sessions, which are recorded and uploaded for reference on the Change11 website. The site also includes an archive of daily newsletters and RSS-feeds of blog posts and tweets from participants.

cMOOCs tend to be learner-centered. People are encouraged to pursue their own interests and link up with others who might help them. But the distributed and free nature of the projects also leads to complaints; participants often find it confusing when they attempt to follow up on all the discussions (the facilitators say one should not try to follow up on *all* the content).

> **Stephen Downes**: This implies a pedagogy that (a) seeks to describe 'successful' networks (as identified by their properties, which I have characterized as diversity, autonomy, openness, and connectivity); and (b) seeks to describe the practices that lead to such networks, both in the individual and in society (which I have characterized as modeling and demonstration (on the part of a teacher) and practice and reflection (on the part of a learner).

## Anatomy of a cMOOC

One example of a MOOC that claims to embody the connectivist theory is change.mooc.ca. The "how it works" section of the site explains what connectivism means in practice. The MOOC organizers developed a number of ways to combine the distributed nature of the discussions with the need for a constantly updated overview and for a federated structure. So, if your team wants to organize an open online course, these are five points to take into consideration:

There is no body of content the participants have to memorize, but the learning results from activities they undertake. The activities are different for each person. A course schedule with suggested reading, assignments for synchronous or asynchronous sessions is provided (e.g. using Google Docs spreadsheets internally, Google Calendar externally; one could also use a wiki), but participants are free to pick and choose what they work on. Normally there is a topic, activities, reading resources and often a guest speaker for each week. One should even reflect upon the question whether a start- and end date are actually needed. It is crucial to explain the particular philosophy of this kind of MOOC, and this right from the outset, because chances are learners will come with expectations informed by their more traditional learning experiences.

1. It is important to discuss the "internal" aspects, such as self-motivation: what do the participants want to achieve, what is their larger goal? And what are their intentions when they select certain activities (rather than other possibilities)? Everyone has her own intended outcome. Suggest that participants meditate on all this and jot down their objectives. And how can they avoid becoming stressed out and getting depressed because they feel they cannot "keep up with all this?" The facilitators should have a good look at these motivations, even if it's impossible to assist every participant individually (for large-scale MOOCs).
2. Ideally, participants should prepare for this course by acquiring the necessary digital skills. Which skills are "necessary" can be decided by the group itself in advance. It's all about selecting, choosing, remixing - also called "curating". There are lots of tools which you can use for this: blogs, social bookmarks, wikis, mindmaps, forums, social dashboards, networks such as Twitter with their possibilities such as hashtags and lists. Maybe these tools are self-evident for some, but not necessarily for all the participants.
3. The course is not located in one place but is distributed across the web: on various blogs and blogging platforms, on

various groups and online networks, on photo- and video-sharing platforms, on mindmaps and other visualization platforms, on various tools for synchronous sessions. This wide variety is in itself an important learning element.

4. There are weekly synchronous sessions (using Blackboard collaborate, or similar group chatting tool). During these sessions, experts and participants give presentations and enter into discussions. Groups of participants also have synchronous meetings at other venues (such as Second Life). Try to plan this well in advance!
5. Many participants highly appreciate efforts to give an overview of the proceedings. Specifically, the Daily Newsletter is a kind of hub, a community newspaper. In that Daily there is also a list of the blog posts mentioning the course-specific tag (e.g. "Change11"), also the tweets with hashtag #change11 are listed in the Daily. Of course, the MOOC has a site where sessions, newsletters and other resources are archived and discussion threads can be read.

From the very beginning of the course, it's necessary to explain the importance of tagging the various contributions, to suggest a hashtag.

For harvesting all this distributed content, Stephen Downes advocates the use of gRSShopper, which is a personal web environment that combines resource aggregation, a personal dataspace, and personal publishing (Downes developed it and would like to build a hosted version - eventually financed via Kickstarter). The gRSShopper can be found on a registration page, which is useful primarily for sending the newsletter. It allows you to organize your online content any way you want, to import content - your own or others' - from remote sites, to remix and repurpose it, and to distribute it as RSS, web pages, JSON data, or RSS feeds.

> **Stephen Downes**: For example, the gRSShopper harvester will harvest a link from a given feed. A person, if he or she has admin privileges, can transform

> this link into a post, adding his or her own comments. The post will contain information about the original link's author and journal. Content in gRSShopper is created and manipulated through the use of system code that allows administrators to harvest, map, and display data, as well as to link to and create their own content. gRSShopper is also intended to act as a fully-fledged publishing tool.

Alternatives for registrations: Google Groups for instance. But specific rules about privacy should be dealt with: what will be the status of the contributions? In this MOOC the status is public and open by default, for Downes this is an important element of the course.

## Technologies

Some MOOCs use Moodle, but Downes dislikes the centralization aspect and it's not as open as it could be, saying "people feel better writing in their own space." Other possibilities: Google Groups, Wordpress, Diigo, Twitter, Facebook page, Second Life; but each course uses different mixtures of the many tools out there. People choose their environment - whether it is WoW or Minecraft. Students use Blogger, WordPress, Tumblr, Posterous as blogging tools.

## RSS harvesting is a key element

Give participants a means to contribute their blogfeed. In "Add a New Feed," Downes explains how to get this structure and additional explanations (via videos) in order to contribute their blog feed. The administrator in this case uses gRSShopper to process the content and put it in a database, process it and send it to other people. Alternatively one can use Google Reader (the list of feeds is available as an OPML file - which can be imported to other platforms). There is also a plug-in for Wordpress that lets you use a

Google Doc spreadsheet for the feeds, then Wordpress for the aggregation). Many other content management systems have RSS harvesting features.

Each individual could run her own aggregator, but Downes offers it as a service. But aggregators are needed, whether individual, centralized or both.

### Specialized harvesting

Using Twitter, Diigo, Delicious, Google Groups, If This Then That (IFTTT) and Feed43 (take ordinary web page and turn it into an RSS feed).

### Synchronous environments

Synchronous platforms include Blackboard Collaborate (used now for Change11); Adobe Connect; Big Blue Button; WizIQ; Fuze; WebX; webcasting; web radio; videoconferencing with Skype or Google Hangout in conjunction with Livestream or ustream.tv. Or take the Skype/Hangout audiostream and broadcast is as webradio. Set up and test ahead of time, but don't hesitate to experiment. Note also, there is a more extensive discussion of real-time tools in another section of the handbook.

### Newsletter or Feeds

Feeds are very important (see earlier remarks about the Daily newsletter). You can use Twitter or a Facebook page, Downes uses email, also creates an RSS version through gRSShopper and sends it through Ifttt.com back to Facebook and Twitter. For the rest of us there is Wordpress, which you can use to create an email news letter. Downs also suggests this handy guide on how to design and build an email newsletter without loosing your mind!

Consider using a content management system and databases to put out specialized pages and the newsletter in an elegant way, but it requires a learning curve. Otherwise, use blogs / wikis.

### The Use of Comments

Participants are strongly encouraged to comment on each others' blogs and to launch discussion threads. By doing so they practice a fundamental social media skill - developing networks by commenting on various places and engaging in conversations. It is important to have activities and get people to be involved rather than sit back. For an in-depth presentation, have a look at Facilitating a Massive Open Online Course by Stephen Downes, in which he focuses on research and survey issues, preparing events, and other essentials.

## Resources

- Change MOOC: How this Course Works
- What is a MOOC (video)
- Success in a MOOC (video)
- Knowledge in a MOOC (video)
- Introduction and invitation (video)

# Part IX

# Resources

CHAPTER 29

# HOW TO PUT PEERAGOGY INTO ACTION

We have been writing the missing manual for peer-produced peer learning – the "Peeragogy Handbook" (peeragogy.org). While building this book, we, ourselves peer learners in this quest, have been mindful of these four questions:

1. *How does a motivated group of self-learners choose a subject or skill to learn?*
2. *How can this group identify and select the best learning resources about that topic?*
3. *How will these learners identify and select the appropriate technology and communications tools and platforms to accomplish their learning goal?*
4. *What does the group need to know about learning theory and practice to put together a successful peer-learning program?*

It is clear to us that the techniques of peer production that have built and continue to improve *Wikipedia* and GNU/Linux have yet to fully demonstrate their power in education. We believe that the *Peeragogy Handbook* can help change that by building a distributed community of peer learners/educators, and a strongly vetted collection of best practices. Our project complements others' work on sites like Wikiversity and P2PU, and builds upon understandings that have developed informally in distributed communities of hobbyists and professionals, as well as in (and beyond) the classrooms of generations of passionate educators. Here, we present Peeragogy in Action, a project guide in four parts. Each part relates to one or more sections of our handbook, and suggests activities to try while you explore peer learning. These activities are designed for flexible use by widely distributed groups, collaborating via a light-weight infrastructure. Participants may be educators, community organizers, designers, hackers, dancers, students, seasoned peeragogues, or first-timers. The guide should be useful for groups who want to build a strong collaboration, as well as to facilitators or theorists who want to hone their practice or approach. Together, we will use our various talents to build effective methods and models for peer produced peer learning. Let's get started!

**Setting the initial challenge and building a framework for accountability among participants is an important starting point.**

*Activity* – Come up with a plan for your work and an agreement, or informal contract, for your group. You can use the suggestions in this guide as a starting point, but your first task is to revise the plan to suit your needs. It might be helpful to ask: What are you interested in learning? What is your primary intended outcome? What problem do you hope to solve? How collaborative does your project need to be? How will the participants' expertise in the topic vary? What sort of support will you and other participants require? What problems won't you solve?

*Technology* – Familiarize yourself with the collaboration tools you intend to use (e.g. WordPress, Git and LaTeX, YouTube, GIMP, a public wiki, a private forum, or something else) and create a first post, edit, or video introducing yourself and your project(s) to others in the worldwide peeragogy community.

*Suggested Resources* – The Peeragogy Handbook, parts I ('Introduction') and II ('Motivation'). You may also want to work through a short lesson called Implementing Paragogy, from the early days before the Peeragogy project was convened. For a succinct theoretical treatment, please refer to our literature review, which we have adapted into a Wikipedia page.

*Further Reading* – Boud, D. and Lee, A. (2005). *'Peer learning' as pedagogic discourse for research education.* Studies in Higher Education, 30(5):501–516.

*Observations from the Peeragogy project* – We had a fairly weak project structure at the outset, which yielded mixed results. One participant said: "I definitely think I do better when presented with a framework or scaffold to use for participation or content development." Yet the same person wrote with enthusiasm about models of entrepreneurship, saying she was "freed of the requirement or need for an entrepreneurial visionary."

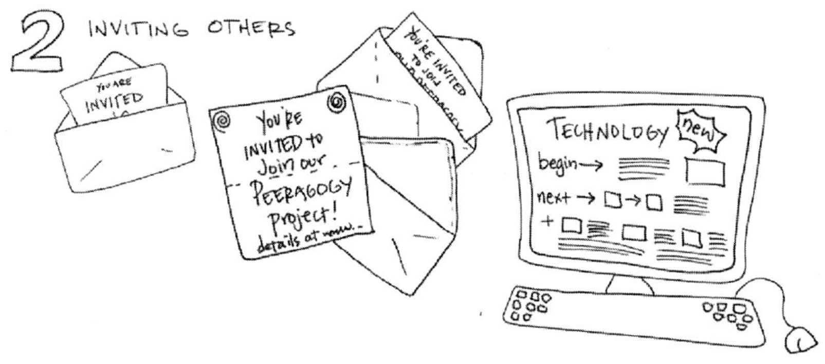


**Other people can support you in achieving your goal and make the work more fun too.**

*Activity* – Write an invitation to someone who can help as a co-facilitator on your project. Clarify what you hope to learn from them and what your project has to offer. Helpful questions to consider as you think about who to invite: What resources are available or missing? What do you already have that you can build on? How will you find the necessary resources? Who else is interested in these kinds of challenges? Go through the these questions again when you have a small group, and come up with a list of more people you'd like to invite or consult with as the project progresses.

*Technology* – Identify tools that could potentially be useful during the project, even if it's new to you. Start learning how to use them. Connect with people in other locales who share similar interests or know the tools.

*Suggested resources* – The Peeragogy Handbook, parts IV ('Convening a Group') and V ('Organizing a Learning Context').

*Recommended Reading* – Schmidt, J. Philipp. (2009). Commons-Based Peer Production and education. Free Culture Research Workshop Harvard University, 23 October 2009.

*Observations from the Peeragogy project* – We used a strategy of "open enrollment." New people were welcome to join the project at any time. We also encouraged people to either stay involved or withdraw; several times over the first year, we required participants to explicitly reaffirm interest in order to stay registered in the forum and mailing list.

**Solidifying your work plan and learning strategy together with concrete measures for 'success' can move the project forward significantly.**

*Activity* – Distill your ideas by writing an essay, making visual sketches, or creating a short video to communicate the unique plans for organization and evaluation that your group will use. By this time, you should have identified which aspects of the project need to be refined or expanded. Dive in!

*Technology* – Take time to mentor others or be mentored by someone, meeting up in person or online. Pair up with someone else and share knowledge together about one or more tools. You can discuss some of the difficulties that you've encountered, or teach a beginner some tricks.

*Suggested resources* – The Peeragogy Handbook, parts VI ('Cooperation'), VII ('Assessment'), and at least some of part II ('Peeragogy in Practice').

*Recommended reading* – Argyris, Chris. "Teaching smart people how to learn." Harvard Business Review 69.3 (1991); and, Gersick, Connie J.G. "Time and transition in work teams: Toward a new model of group development." Academy of Management Journal 31.1 (1988): 9-41.

*Observations from the Peeragogy project* – Perhaps one of the most important roles in the Peeragogy project was the role of the 'Wrapper', who prepared and circulated weekly summaries of forum activity. This helped people stay informed about what was happening in the project even if they didn't have time to read the forums. We've also found that small groups of people who arrange their own meetings are often the most productive.

**Wrap up the project with a critical assessment of progress and directions for future work. Share any changes to this syllabus that you think would be useful for future peeragogues!**

*Activity* – Identify the main obstacles you encountered. What are some goals you were not able to accomplish yet? Did you foresee these challenges at the outset? How did this project resemble or differ from others you've worked on? How would you do things differently in future projects? What would you like to tackle next?

*Writing* – Communicate your reflection case. Prepare a short written or multimedia essay, dealing with your experiences in this course. Share the results by posting it where others in the broader Peeragogy project can find it.

*'Extra credit'* – Contribute back to one of the other organisations or projects that helped you on this peeragogical journey. Think about what you have to offer. Is it a bug fix, a constructive critique, pictures, translation help, PR, wiki-gnoming or making a cake? Make it something special, and people will remember you and thank you for it.

*Suggested resources* – The Peeragogy Handbook, parts VIII ('Technologies, Services, and Platforms') and IX ('Resources').

*Recommended reading* – Stallman, Richard. "Why software should be free" (1992).

*Observations from the Peeragogy project* – When we were deciding how to license our work, we decided to use CC0, emphasizing 're-usability' and hoping that other people would come and remix the handbook. At the moment, we're still waiting to see the first remix edition, but we're confident that it will come along in due course. Maybe you'll be the one who makes it!

## Micro-Case Study: The Peeragogy Project, Year 1

Since its conception in early 2012, the Peeragogy Project has collected over 3700 comments in our discussion forum, and over 200 pages of expository text in the handbook. It has given contributors a new way of thinking about things together. However, the project has not had the levels of engagement that should be possible, given the technology available, the global interest in improving education, and the number of thoughtful participants who expressed interest. We hope that the handbook and this accompanying syllabus will provide a seed for a new phase of learning, with many new contributors and new ideas drawn from real-life applications.

## Micro-Case Study: The Peeragogy Project, Year 2

10 new handbook contributors joined in the project's second year. We've begun a series of weekly Hangouts on Air that have brought in many additional discussants, all key people who can help to fulfil peeragogy's promise. The handbook has been considerably improved through edits and discussion. The next step for us is putting this work into action in the *Peeragogy Accelerator.*

## Micro-Case Study: The Peeragogy Project, Year 3

We published our plans as "Building the Peeragogy Accelerator", presenting it at OER14 and inviting feedback. In the run up to this, we had been very active creating additional abstracts and submitting them to conferences. However, despite our efforts we failed to recruit any newcomers for the trial run of the Accelerator. Even so, piloting the Accelerator with some of our own projects worked reasonably well,[1] but we decided to focus on the handbook in the second half of the year. As the project's line-up shifted, participants reaffirmed the importance of having "no camp counsellors." In the last quarter of 2014, we created the workbook that is now presented in Part I, as a quickstart guide to peeragogy.

## Micro-Case Study: The Peeragogy Project, Year 4

We didn't publish a new version of the *Handbook* last year, so the new Third Edition catches up on two years of work. One of our main activities this year was a thorough revision of the pattern catalog in Part III of the book. We used the revised format to create a "distributed roadmap" for the Peeragogy project – featured in Chapter 7 of the new Third Edition. We've continued to meet just about every week for Hangouts.[2] Prompted by a malware attack on our old Wordpress site, we finally got around to moving peeragogy.org to Github, which gives us a new way to collaborate.

[1] For an overview, see http://is.gd/up_peeragogy_accelerator.
[2] http://is.gd/peeragogy_videos

CHAPTER 30

# SOME LANDMARKS FROM THE LIFE OF PEERAGOGY

## Feedback from two novice course organizers

*Before the Peeragogy project as such was convened, two of us realised that "peer produced peer learning" could benefit from further theoretical and practical development. Here is a summary of our early thoughts as volunteer course organizers at the Peer-2-Peer University (P2PU):*

▸ Our best experiences as course organizers happened when we were committed to working through the material ourselves. Combining this with gently prompting peers to follow through on their commitments could go a long way towards keeping engagement at a reasonable level – but this only works when commitments are somewhat clear in the first place.

▸ It is typical for online communities to have strictly enforced community norms. It would be helpful to have a concise discussion of these available, together with up to date information on "best practices" for organizers and participants. The current Course Design Handbook provides one starting point, but it falls short of being a complete guide to P2PU.

▸ In a traditional university, there are typically a lot of ways to resolve problems without dropping out. P2PU's new "Help Desk" could help with this issue – if people use it.

▸ P2PU would have to work hard to use anything but "participation" as a proxy value for "learning." In terms of broader issues of quality control, one serious thought is for P2PU core members (including staff) to use the platform to organize their activities – entirely in the open.

▸ It is our firm belief that P2PU should work on a public roadmap that leads from now up to the point where the vision is achieved. Both vision and roadmap should be revised as appropriate.

## The "FLOK Doc": Widespread Peeragogy

*In 2013, Ecuador launched the Free/Libre/Open Knowledge Society Project to facilitate the transition to a* 'buen saber', *or* 'good knowledge' *society, which is an extension of the official strategy towards a* 'buen vivir'*-based society. The Peeragogy project contributed a brief to help develop this plan. Here are some highlights:*

Ecuador has a law about free software and open knowledge (*Decreto 1014*, launched 2008). Article 32 of the *Ley orgánica de Educación Superior* makes open source software mandatory for higher education. Public universities are building their own OER repositories. What peeragogy can offer are are working methods for co-producing relevant Open Educational Resources on a wider scale. As such, peeragogy is especially relevant to the goals and working methods of the *Human Capabilities* stream of the FLOK project, but here are some ways it could affect the other streams:

▸ *Commons-oriented Productive Capacities* will require people to learn new ways of working. Can we start to build a peeragogical "extension school", by collaborating on a new handbook about sustainable agricultural techniques?

▸ *Social Infrastructure and Institutional Innovation* will require collaboration between many different agencies, local enterprises, and global organizations. Can peeragogy help these groups cooperate effectively? Coauthoring a handbook about inter-agency cooperation could help.

▸ *Hardware and Connectivity* needs to be connected to documentation and active, participatory, support that shows

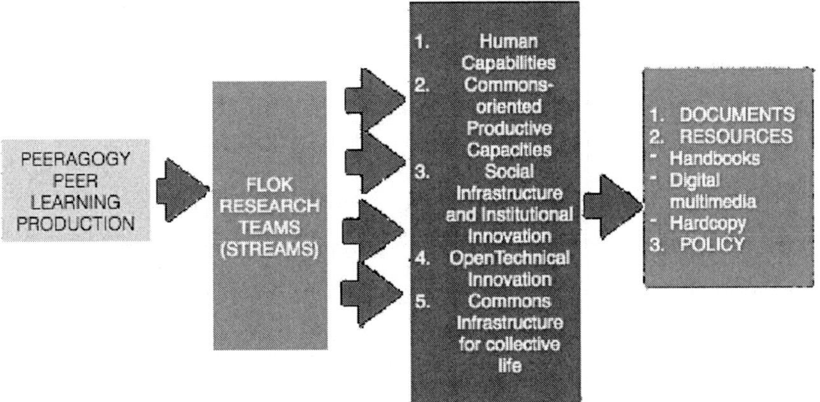


Peeragogy in relation to the FLOK Society Project

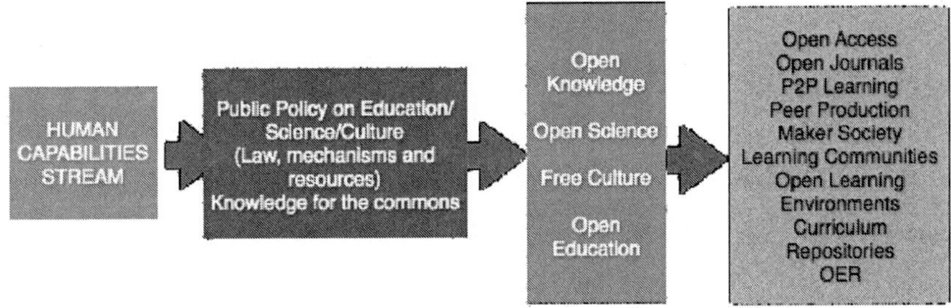


Peeragogy is especially relevant to the goals and working methods of the Human Capabilities Stream of the FLOK Society Project

how to use and adapt new technologies to our use cases.

▸ *Commons' Infrastructure for Collective Life* could co-develop along with a pattern language that shows how to interconnect elements of knowledge and practical solutions that are (re)generative of the commons and relevant to learners' needs.

## New strategies for "good faith collaboration"

*We're strongly in favor of the Wikimedia Foundation's mission, "to empower and engage people around the world to collect and develop educational content under a free license or in the public domain, and to disseminate it effectively and globally." We hope peeragogy can contribute to this and other free/open efforts to constructively reshape the way education works in the future. Some shared values:*

▸ *Neutral POV*: Pretty much anyone can write an article for the *Peeragogy Handbook* on anything related to peer learning and peer production. We'll help review and edit to make the work shine. Rather than requiring each individual article to be neutral, we strive for overall comprehensiveness.

▸ *Free content*: We've taken the radical step of putting material in the handbook into the public domain, which means that anyone can reuse material in the handbook for any purpose whatsoever, without asking permission or even giving us attribution. The reason being: we want to make re-use, application, and extension of this work as simple as possible.

▸ *Respect and civility*: We strive to focus on learning. If someone disagrees with a given choice, we remember that in true dialogue there are no right or wrong answers and no one in charge. If someone seems to be frustrated with the way the project is going, we ask why and attempt to learn from them about what we could change – in order to learn more.

▸ *No firm rules*: The project roadmap is fluid, and our understanding of the idea of "peeragogy" is revised and extended as we go. The living patterns we catalog (in Part III) aren't prescriptive but they do seem to reappear with variation across different learning scenarios. We don't have a fixed platform or leadership structure, but use whatever tools and teams seem most suitable for the purpose at hand.

CHAPTER 31

# RECOMMENDED READING

## "Good faith collaboration"


1. Reagle, J. M. (2010). Good faith collaboration: The culture of Wikipedia, MIT Press.


## Writings about fun and boredom


1. Kano, J. (1995/2013). The Contribution of Judo to Education.

2. Pale King, unfinished novel, by David Foster Wallace

3. On the Poverty of Student Life, by Mustapha Khayati


## The structure of learning

Check out work by Bruce Tuckman, Gilly Salmon, Ken Wilber, Martin Oliver, Gráinne Conole, Ruth Deakin-Crick, Howard Gardner, and Mihaly Csíkszentmihályi.

## Motivation


1. Simon Sinek, Start With Why: How Great Leaders Inspire Everyone To Take Action, Penguin Books, 2011


## Case Study: 5PH1NX


1. Senge, Peter. "The fifth discipline: The art and science of the learning organization." *New York: Currency Doubleday* (1990).

## Alexandrian Design Patterns

1. Article, "Manifesto 1991" by Christopher Alexander, Progressive Architecture, July 1991, pp. 108–112, provides a brief summary of Alexander's ideas in the form of a critique of mainstream architecture. Many of the same sorts of critical points would carry over to mainstream education. Some highlights are excerpted here.

2. The Origins of Pattern Theory, the Future of the Theory, And The Generation of a Living World, Christopher Alexander's talk at the 1996 ACM Conference on Object-Oriented Programs, Systems, Languages and Applications (OOPSLA)

## On Newcomers

1. OpenHatch.org, "an open source community aiming to help newcomers find their way into free software projects."

2. Why do newcomers abandon open source software projects? (sildes by Igor Steinmacher and coauthors)

## Antipatterns

1. The Sapir-Whorf Hypothesis

2. Bourdieu's notion of "symbolic violence".

## SWATs

1. Cavallo, David. "Emergent design and learning environments: Building on indigenous knowledge." IBM Systems Journal 39.3.4 (2000): 768-781.

## Convening a Group

1. Engeström, Y. (1999). Innovative learning in work teams: Analyzing cycles of knowledge creation in practice. In Y.

Engeström, R. Miettinen & R.-L-. Punamäki (Eds.), *Perspectives on activity theory*, (pp. 377-404). Cambridge, UK: Cambridge University Press

2. Gersick, C. (1988). Time and transition in work teams: Toward a new model of group development. *Academy of Management Journal* 31 (Oct.): 9-41.
3. Mimi Ito's observations about manga fan groups co-learning Japanese
4. Rheingold U, MindAmp groups
5. Shneiderman, B. (2007). Creativity support tools: accelerating discovery and innovation. *Commun. ACM* 50, 12 (December 2007), 20-32.
6. David de Ugarte, Phyles. (Summary) (Book)
7. Scheidel, T. M., & Crowell, L. (1964). Idea development in small discussion groups. *Quarterly Journal of Speech*, 50, 140-145.
8. Scheidel, T. M., & Crowell, L. (1979), *Discussing and Deciding - A Desk Book for Group Leaders and Members*, Macmillan Publishing
9. Ozturk and Simsek, "Of Conflict in Virtual Learning Communiities in the Context of a Democratic Pedagogy: A paradox or sophism?," in *Proceedings of the Networked Learning Conference, 2012, Maastricht.* Video or text.
10. Paragogy Handbook, How to Organize a MOOC
11. Cathy Davidson et al., How a Class Becomes a Community

## K-12 Peeragogy

**For pointers to tools for your classroom, check out:**

- Richard Byrne

- Sylvia Tolisano
- Caitlin Tucker
- Vicki Davis

**How to develop your PLN:**

- Degrees of Connected Teaching by Rodd Lucier
- TeachThought

**Theory & philosophy of connnected learning for classroom transformation:**

- David Truss
- Steven Downes
- Will Richardson

## Adding Structure with Activities

1. The d.school Bootcamp Bootleg (CC-By-NC-SA) includes lots of fun activities to try. Can you crack the code and define new ones that are equally cool?

2. Puzio, R. S. (2005). "On free math and copyright bottlenecks." *Free Culture and the Digital Library Symposium Proceedings.*

## Co-Facilitation

1. Peer Education: Training of Trainers Manual; UN Interagency Group on Young Peoples Health

2. Co Facilitating: Advantages & Potential Disadvantages. J. Willam Pfeifer and John E Johnes

3. Summary of John Heron's model of the role of facilitators

4. Carl Rogers, Core Conditions and Education, Encyclopedia of Informal Education
5. Peer Mediation, Study Guides and Strategies
6. Co-Facilitation: The Advantages and Challenges, Canadian Union of Public Employees
7. Bohemia Interactive Community Wiki Guidelines
8. Barrett-Lennard, G. T. (1998) *Carl Roger's Helping System. Journey and Substance*, London: Sage
9. 5 Pillars of Wikipedia, from Wikipedia
10. *Training the Force* (2002) US Army Field Manual #FM 7-0 (FM 25-100)
11. Learning Reimagined: Participatory, Peer, Global, Online, by Howard Rheingold
12. Research Gate is a network dedicated to science and research, in which members connect, collaborate and discover scientific publications, jobs and conferences.
13. Creating and Facilitating Peer Support Groups, by The Community Tool Box
14. Facilitation Tips, by Villanova University
15. Herding Passionate Cats: The Role of Facilitator in a Peer Learning, by Pippa Buchanan
16. Reflective Peer Facilitation: Crafting Collaborative Self-Assessment, by Dale Vidmar, Southern Oregon University Library
17. Effective Co-Facilitation, by Everywoman's Center, University of Massachussetts
18. "Teaching smart people how to learn" by Chris Argyris, Harvard Business Review 69.3, 1991; also published in expanded form as a book with the same name.

## Assessment


1. Morgan, C. and M. O'Reilly. (1999). Assessing Open and distance learners. London: Kogan Page Limited.

2. Schmidt, J. P., Geith, C., Håklev, S. and J. Thierstein. (2009). Peer-To-Peer Recognition of Learning in Open Education. *International Review of Research in Open and Distance Learning*. Volume 10, Number 5.

3. L.S. Vygotsky: Mind in Society: Development of Higher Psychological Processes

4. Reijo Miettinen and Jaakko Virkkunen, Epistemic Objects, Artifacts and Organizational Change, *Organization,* May 2005, 12: 437-456.


## Technologies, Services, and Platforms


1. Irene Greif and Sunil Sarin (1987): Data Sharing in Group Work, ACM Transactions on Office Information Systems, vol. 5, no. 2, April 1987, pp. 187-211.

2. Irene Greif (ed.) (1988): Computer-Supported Cooperative Work: A Book of Readings, San Mateo, CA: Morgan Kaufman.

3. Irene Greif (1988): Remarks in panel discussion on "CSCW: What does it mean?", CSCW '88. Proceedings of the Conference on Computer-Supported Cooperative Work, September 26-28, 1988, Portland, Oregon, ACM, New York, NY.

4. Kammersgaard, J., Four Different Perspectives on Human-Computer Interaction. International Journal of Man-Machine Studies 28(4): 343-362 (1988)

5. DeSanctis, G. and Poole, M. S. 1994, 'Capturing the complexity in advanced technology use: Adaptive structuration theory', Organisation Science, vol. 5, no. 2, p. 121-47.

6. Norman, D. A. 1986, 'Cognitive engineering', in Norman, D. A. and Draper, S. W., (eds) User Centered System Design: New Perspectives on Human-Computer Interaction, pp. 31-61. Hillsdale, NJ: Lawrence Erlbaum and Associates.

7. Vessey, I. and Galletta, D. 1991, 'Cognitive fit: An empirical study of information acquisition', Information Systems Research, vol. 2, no. 1, pp. 63-84.

### Real-Time Meetings

1. Howard Rheingold's webconferencing bookmarks on Delicious.

### Additional Tips from an open source perspective

Care of User:Neophyte on the Teaching Open Source wiki.

1. The Art of Community

2. Open Advice

3. The Open Source Way

## Forums

1. Rheingold, H. Why use forums? *Social Media Classroom.*

2. Rheingold, H. (1998). The Art of Hosting Good Conversations Online.

3. Gallagher, E. J. (2006). Guidelines for Discussion Board Writing. Lehigh University.

4. Gallagher, E.J. (2009). Shaping a culture of conversation. The discussion board and beyond. The Academic Commons.

5. Academic Technology Center. (2010). Improving the Use of Discussion Boards. Worcester Polytechnic Institute.

## Paragogy

1. Corneli, J. (2010). Implementing Paragogy, on *Wikiversity.*

2. Corneli, J. and C. Danoff. (2010/2013). *Paragogy.net.*

## Learning vs Training

1. Hart, J. (April 20th, 2012). Is it time for a BYOL (Bring Your Own Learning) strategy for your organization? *Learning in the Social Space. Jane Hart's Blog.*

## PLNs

1. Rheingold, H. (2010). Shelly Terrell: Global Netweaver, Curator, PLN Builder. *DML Central.*

2. Richardson, W. and R. Mancabelli. (2011). Personal Learning Networks: Using the Power of Connection to Transform Education. Bloomington, IN: Solution Tree Press.

3. Howard Rheingold's PLN links on Delicious

## Connectivism in Practice — How to Organize a MOOC (Massive Open Online Class)

1. Downes & Siemens MOOC site

2. What Connectivism Is by Stephen Downes

3. An Introduction to Connective Knowledge by Stephen Downes

4. Facilitating a Massive Open Online Course, by Stephen Downes

5. gRSShopper

6. Connectivism: A Learning Theory for the Digital Age by George Siemens

7. A Connectivism Glossary
8. Rhizomes and Networks by George Siemens
9. Rhizomatic Education: Community as Curriculum by Dave Cormier
10. Knowing Knowledge, a book by George Siemens
11. Net Smart, Howard Rheingold (about internal and external literacies for coping with the 'always on' digital era)
12. Massive Open Online Courses: Setting Up (StartToMOOC, Part 1)
13. The MOOC guide

### And, a word list for your inner edu-geek

You can read about all of these things on Wikipedia.

1. Constructivism
2. Social constructivism
3. Radical constructivism
4. Enactivism
5. Constructionism
6. Connectivism

CHAPTER 32

# STYLE GUIDE

*This is a How-To Handbook.*

## Keep it short

The easiest sections to read are those that are shorter and include some kind of visual (video or image) and have some personal connection (i.e. they tell a story). For anything longer, break it up into sub-pages, add visuals, make sure each sub-page is accessible to someone (who is it?). Think clearly of this reader, talk to them.

## Make it clear

We'll illustrate this point by example. The original full title of the book was "The Peeragogy Handbook: A resource for self-organizing self-learners". But "self-organizing" is a technical term, and "self-learner" is a confusing neologism. We shouldn't use technical terms unless we explain them. So we really shouldn't use it in the first sentence or paragraph, or title, of the book because we'll scare people off or confuse them. If we want to explain what "self-organization" means and why it is relevant for peeragogy, then we can take a chapter to do that much later on in the book. At the same time, we shouldn't try to "say the same thing in a simpler way." We should try to get rid of the technical concept completely and see what's left. The easiest thing to do in such cases is to delete the sentence completely and start over: when in doubt, speak plainly.

## Don't overdo it with bullet points

Text can be very hard to read when there are more than a few bullet points included. Numbered lists should also be used sparingly. It also seems that when many disjointed bullet points appear, sometimes the author is really just indexing the main points that are presented better in someone else's narrative. Therefor, consider replacing an entire bulleted list with a reference to someone else's book/webpage/chapter. In today's hyperlinked world, it's easy enough for the reader to go elsewhere to get good content (and indeed, we should make it easy for them to find the best treatments around!). It is not very pleasant to have to *read* a taxonomy.

## Include activities

When reading, editing or otherwise working your way through the book, please make note of any activities or exercises that come to mind, and share them. We're always striving to be more practical and applicable.

## Don't be overly chatty

In our efforts to escape from academia-speak and simplify the text in the handbook, it's important to make sure we are not heading towards the other extreme – being too conversational. When we're having a conversation with someone, we tend to pepper our ideas with transitional or pivotal phrases ("In any event," "With that said," "As I mentioned elsewhere," etc.) that help to keep the talk flowing. We also go off on brief tangents before making our way back to the main topic, and sometimes express ourselves in run-on sentences. While this is perfectly natural in speech, it can be confusing and complex in written text. Let's strive for the perfect balance of simple yet professional writing.

## Additional style bonus points

- Avoid double lines after paragraphs; this is a leftover from the age of typewriters and can create "rivers" of white space.

- Capitalize the first word of each item in a bulleted list, especially if items include a verb form (this list is an example!). Punctuate uniformly.
- Capitalize the first word of headings and subheadings; lower case all others.

## Format your HTML nicely

We need to be able to process the content from this Wordpress site and turn it into various formats like LaTeX and EPUB. Our automated tools work much better if pages are formatted with simple and uniform HTML markup. Some key points:

- Mark up your links: use The Peeragogy Handbook instead of http://peeragogy.org. It's best if the link text is somewhat descriptive.
- Use a numbered list to format your references (see Convening a Group for one example of an article that gets this right!)
- Use Heading 2 and Heading 3 tags to mark up sections, not **bold** text. If you use bold or italics in your paragraphs, you should **check** that the markup *is actually correct.* It should exactly surround the words that you're marking up – `<em>like this</em>` – and it should not include extra spaces around marked up words – `<em> NOT like this </em>`.
- Be aware that Wordpress does not always add paragraph tags to your paragraphs.
- Wordpress also tries to replace straight quote marks with "smart quotes", but it sometimes doesn't achieve the aim. If you notice weird quotemarks (especially in the PDF version), you can add smart quote marks by hand.

CHAPTER 33

# LICENSE/WAIVER

These materials are made available under the terms of Creative Commons 0 copyright waiver instead of a "traditional" copyleft license. We the undersigned agree to the following, wherein "this work" refers to "The Peeragogy Handbook" and all other content posted on peeragogy.org or the original collaboratory site, http://socialmediaclassroom.com/host/peeragogy.

**I hereby waive all copyright and related or neighboring rights together with all associated claims and causes of action with respect to this work to the extent possible under the law.**

Signed:

- Bryan Alexander
- Paul Allison
- Elisa Armendáriz
- Régis Barondeau
- Doug Breitbart
- George Brett
- Suz Burroughs
- Joseph Corneli
- Jay Cross
- Charles Jeffrey Danoff
- Karen Beukema Einstein
- Julian Elve
- María Fernanda Arenas
- James Folkestad
- John Graves
- Kathy Gill
- Matthew Herschler
- Gigi Johnson

- Anna Keune
- Kyle Larson
- Roland Legrand
- Amanda Lyons
- Lisa Snow MacDonald
- Dorotea Mar
- Christopher Tillman Neal
- Ted Newcomb
- Stephanie Parker
- Miguel Ángel Pérez Álvarez
- Charlotte Pierce
- David Preston
- Howard Rheingold
- Paola Ricaurte
- Verena Roberts
- Stephanie Schipper
- Fabrizio Terzi
- Geoff Walker

Note that this waiver does not apply to other works by the above authors, including works linked to from peeragogy.org. It also does not apply to embedded content drawn from other sites and included for the reader's convenience.

Future contributors: Note also that we will require a similar copyright waiver agreement. That said, the waiver also means that you are free to do essentially whatever you like with the content in your own work! Have fun!

### How we came to this decision

These Creative Commons license options were proposed by various members of the community:

- *CC Zero* - public domain; no restrictions for downstream users

- *CC By-SA* - requires downstream users to include attribution and to license their work in the same way
- *CC By-SA-NC* - requires downstream users to include attribution, to license their work in the same way and disallows any commercial use of the content

After a brief discussion, no one was in favor of restricting downstream users, so we decided to go with CC0. We agreed that we would get enough "credit" by having our names on peeragogy.org. In connection with this discussion, we agreed that we would work on ways to explicitly build "reusability" into the handbook content.